LUV PSALM

by

Daniel P. Hochreiter

To Big Pine Donny

My Friend

Acknowledgments

These are the people who have in some way touched me and, in turn, my writing. Thank you all.

Mom and Dad. For your love and showing me what family truly is or can be. The family you created might be a bit dysfunctional at times, though we all know because of you both what love is. I may not always like all of you, but I will always love you.

My fellow campers that I now consider my other family. I repeat, I may not always like all of you........

My sister Dee (Sandy Wommeldorf) and Shawni (Joan) Kingsbury. Dee and Shawni were the only ones I had shared what depths of my soul writing took me to, yet they both still said "go for it" when I told them I was going to try again to write.

Joann (the owner and matriarch of The Fishing Lodge). I can only hope your hard work and diligence have made you realize your dreams. I also want you to know how many of us have realized our dreams because of your endeavors.

Dr. Dan Woperer, a former customer and now someone I consider a friend. I shared my first draft of this book with him and he proclaimed that he "liked it." I found out that he was actually a retired medical doctor and was then teaching at the University of Rochester. He now teaches at Duke University in North Carolina. When I gave him and his wife, Chrissie, the first round of my book, he came back with his thoughts. They were brutally honest and I never had received that before. He was kind in his words, though... honest

Ouch, the truth hurts! I sat down and actually read my words for the first time, and they all changed. I do thank him for that. I have a feeling he is an amazing teacher.

Charles (Chuck) Bailey, a teacher. Mr. Bailey told me to put a story I had told into written words, and I still don't know whether to thank him or kick him in the balls. Not only did he give me encouragement to write, but he gave me a book of poems he'd written. I told him the next day, "I don't fucking get it," and he thanked me for my honesty. Within a week I had written seventy-plus poems.

This one's for you, Chuck.

* * *

A Teacher's Gift

A story told to words of praise
To a stranger soon to change
The story retold in written words
From that stranger soon to change
A spark ignited turned into flames
For that stranger that soon changed
That stranger was always there
The stranger was within
The only words that teacher spoke
Words that changed my life
"Try something new."

* * *

I know that a rose is a rose and violets are blue and Humpty Dumpty got more than a few cracks in his ass. My poem might be dumb, but aren't all poems? "A Teachers Gift" is a testament to *all* those who encourage others to "try something new."

We all teach, whether through words or actions. Sometimes others learn through our lack of words or our inactions.

To my dear ole dad, who has moved on to the next life, thanks, Pops. This one's for you.

* * *

I reached so high above me
For that hand so filled with love
We walked along
No words were spoken
Though volumes were exchanged
My joy came from within his shadow
His shadow from my sunshine.

* * *

Daniel's Tree Service, Tim Travis, Todd Jackson.

To Santa. I am being a good boy?
To *my* God (you find your own).

* * *

And so let the story of a few days and a few memories I'd like to share with you begin.

Introduction

I had written a story about a fishing experience that, for whatever reason, several papers had deemed worthy enough to include along with those articles written by writers who actually had some concept of what they were doing.

I could only imagine that it had to have been a slow week and they needed space to fill. Or just maybe... I had discovered something that had lain dormant within me all the time?

I am just a someone who works a lot, and I hope that you will allow me to share with you a few moments of my life that I enjoyed with someone else.

Regardless of the reason, my experience was really in print, and having never before attempted writing an experience, the feeling of seeing my article in a magazine was quite a heady one to say the least.

Can you say ecstatic?

Holy shit!

I was now a writer!

Ah yes, a star was born.

Please do not be too humbled in my presence, and I in kind will seek to remain my same old humble self.

A novel was developing in my mind and rapidly finding its way onto paper. I thought I was soon to become an author.

The following year I was returning to the same place that had spawned my newfound creativity to continue my foray into that world of writing, a place where my mind could wander free of the concerns and the desires of others, a place where I wasn't bothered—or maybe didn't care—by customers who had a fifty-year-old tree on the property they'd owned for thirty-five years and that they suddenly had to have removed immediately.

I am self-employed, owning a tree service company. I take care of others' desires more so than my own needs or wants. I had found a place in the Florida Keys where nothing really mattered other than what I was doing at the moment, a place where I hoped to complete that novel.

However, the story that had seemed so clear and relevant in my mind, and easy to write the previous year, suddenly seemed pretty mundane as I began to enjoy my surroundings and the people in it. I was *forcing* words onto paper in an attempt to find that magic again.

My writing fell by the wayside, along with my desire to write. Instead, I found myself spending my time with a person who was just kinda fun to talk with.

This person I came to find inspiring, not so much by what he'd accomplished in life, but by how he lived through what most people would consider a death sentence and a reason to dwell on the "what ifs" of a life with a foreseeable end that was getting closer every day. I now found myself writing about our friendship.

I thought I would title this story *Coffee with Sam*. That title basically said it all: coffee with a newfound friend named Sam and the conversations we shared—old stories, new friends, and a cup of coffee that started our day.

This was the basis for our relationship and my story—two guys sharing old memories and old stories, and in the process, creating a few new ones and new friends, something that in my world I don't experience anymore. I don't seem to take the time to appreciate people, other than the few moments I share with them while discussing the business at hand, even though those few moments are usually the highlight of my day.

The book completed, I let family and friends critique my writings. Too often the response came back the same: "Dan, I like the story. It seems to be a lot like *Tuesdays with Maury.*"

I had asked for people's response, though I guess I was only looking for their praise. I wanted to hear, "This is wonderful." More than a few times they said to try a different title.

I had gone as far with my book as I could. I had rewritten it all too many times. A customer, Rose, told me that her husband, Rick, edited books. I had left my book on my desk for too long and it was time to hand it off to someone that could at least edit.

Rick and Rose Taubold: Rick made some suggestions; Rose read. Together they gave me a little insight. It was what I had been looking for.

I began to fantasize what an actual publisher might say...

* * *

After a whole lot of attempts to find a publisher, my book finds its way into the hands of one that seems truly interested, and I receive a call from a Mr. Winthrop.

He begins with an introduction of both himself and the firm he represents.

"Mr. Hochreiter, my name is Bartholomew T. Winthrop III, and I am calling on behalf of a company interested in your book. In actuality, I own it along with several other companies, and I would love to sit down with you and discuss the possibilities of putting your story into print.

"It's a good story, Daniel, though I was thinking that, between the content and the title, it seems to be along the same lines of Tuesdays with Maury." He continues, or rather tries to continue, "I was thinking—"

I never give him a chance to say what I've heard before. I stop him in midsentence. Sam was a man that was busy living. He loved every minute of his life and enjoyed everything and everyone he came into contact with, and this idiot was not about to change my title that basically said the reason and the basis of our relationship.

"I know what you're going to say, Mr. Winthrop, and this is what I have to say to you: Fuck Maury. Fuck Tuesdays—and you know what?—Fuck you too, Bart."

I hang up the phone and it immediately begins to ring, though I ignore it, knowing it is Bart.

If nothing else, Bart the Third is a persistent bastard. The phone keeps on ringing until I finally shut it off.

I turn the phone back on the following day and am immediately rewarded with it ringing, a call from, who else? The one and only Bartholomew T. Three.

"Dan, let me explain. The story you have written is wonderful and I was just making a suggestion that maybe you would consider—"

I cut him short again. I realize that I am just being bullheaded, as I'm prone to be. I like my title and Ole Bart seems like a turd that is only a businessman, and I assume with a name like that, he has been given not just his title but a sense of entitlement.

"Looky here, Mr. Winthrop. I think you might be right, and I really do not wish to take anything away from Sam and this story. I will indeed change the title. Let's make it Coffee with Sam, every day but Tuesday."

I hang up the phone and know that I am just being stubborn, and so the title of my book has changed.

To you, Bart Three, the only thing I can say is "Bite my rosy red ass!"

After reading my Introduction, Ole Bart informed me, "Dan, it is actually Tuesdays with Morrie, not Tuesdays with Maury." He spells every letter of both Morrie and Maury out.

His tone is smug and I say nothing, letting him feel good about knowing more than me.

I said my piece earlier with Bart Number Three and what I thought of his feelings, and the fact that he called me back was good enough for me.

* * *

And so the title changes.

Chapter 1

LuV I sAm

It was the early eighties and I was in my early twenties.

It was such a wonderful time in my life, as it is in most I suppose, being both young and naive, though I do think (or hope) that's a trait of youth that most of us experience.

I had a bonus as well.

I was in love.

To be innocent is to believe in all of life's possibilities. The world was what we wanted it to be. The world perceived was all we knew; it was our reality.

The future was just that, and as far as I was concerned, or as most that are young, the future was a distant thing that was of little or no concern at all.

Today was at hand, and the tomorrows were a long way off.

Only the present mattered, but of course time would erode all that away, taking both youth and innocence and, at least for me, my current love, and alas, the most precious commodity of all that we are born with: naiveté.

As we grow older, imagination changes into reality; life gets in the way of our dreams. I was still young and dumb and innocent, and ignorance truly is bliss. Once innocence is lost, the world around us seems to change as well. The world we perceived turns into the reality of the life we live.

I think man is the only creature that expects tomorrow to be better, or that even thinks about tomorrow or the future at all.

I suppose that I still refuse to grow up. I tend to say what's on my mind. I say things that make others smile or laugh. I try to invoke thought, or at least a look of "what the hell is he talking about?"

Laugh with me or at me. I don't care just as long as you laugh. It's all good and we both win.

I really do enjoy people, and trust them at their word. Yes, I have been proven wrong time and again, though in the end I figure it's their loss, not mine.

Anyways, I still saw the world as I wanted it to be, and perception, after all, is reality within our own minds.

It was January in New York, where the winter tends to be a bit too long, the weather a little too cold, and the sunshine a whole lotta too rare.

Some friends of mine (as well as my future wife), who were all truly good people, decided to take a break from the doldrums of a New York winter. Our destination was the island of Jamaica, in the Caribbean, a tropical paradise.

Arriving in Montego Bay, we were immediately greeted by the locals at the airport, selling their wares. Even before we could leave, they all but accosted us with the local produce. Their "wares" was probably the most exported product from their country: the ganja, the weed—

or as law enforcement calls it—marijuana. I think I was quite happy with our choice of a vacation place. I think that anyone under the age of sixty, or maybe even under eighty, who visits this country samples that produce, at least when I went and I hope still do.

Making our way through the mayhem of those hawking their product, we found the van that waited to take us to our hotel in the village of Negril, on the westernmost part of the island.

The place we stayed at was The Tigress, a motel, or rather a group of cottages that were just across the road from the ocean. The owner was called "Papa" by anyone and everyone, and he made sure that everything was in order. Our comfort was a major concern of his, and that translated into dollars, which I'm sure was his real concern.

It was long before the Corporate World had figured out how to take advantage of this tropical wonderland and those just looking for a good time.

The all-inclusive deals—where everything is provided for one flat price without ever having to leave the sanctuary of the sponsor's grounds— were still a thing of the future.

For us it was paradise. Our sanctuary was anything and everything we cared to explore, whether on our own or with the help of others.

Our package deal was a hotel room for a hundred dollars a week. It even had a bar and three seats.

Nothing more. Nothing less.

We were left to our own devices. There was no scheduled entertainment or meals supplied, and that was just fine by us. We were in paradise after all: good rum, good food, good people.

And great marijuana.

It was paradise on a budget.

Our only mode of transportation was our youth and all the energy that comes with it. Our feet and a good pair of shoes took us anyplace we cared to go. Everything we needed or wanted was within walking distance, a few hundred feet or a mile plus.

The ocean was just across the road from our room. There was no beach. The shoreline was nothing but rock—or more appropriately, coral. More often than not, we'd go out snorkeling from the front of our place. Sometimes we'd go to the beach that was maybe a half mile away.

The beach had sand and tourists, who were bathed in oil and lying about, their only goal seeming to be to bake their flesh. They would sit on the beach in their chairs and do basically nothing other than collect the rays of the sun. To many, I think the best part of their vacation would be their return to their lily-white friends showing their tan lines and exclaiming the beauty of the tropics, though I think that the only thing they experienced was the sun and a few restaurants and their ignorance of the future of weathered flesh and cancerous tumors.

Tan lines for some are the only thing they really cared to bring back with them—no stories of the beauty of the vibrant colors of the flowers, or of the lush tropics that rose above, not the warmth of the people that lived there nor the memory of a hummingbird feasting on a flower outside their room.

Memories should be stories to share with others about experiences. Memories may fade, but they last. Tans don't.

We were all young, and our only goal was to experience all that Jamaica had to offer, both the beauty of the land and the beauty of the people. It was truly a tropical paradise both above and below the sea.

Snorkeling from the shores that were just across from our rooms was fun, and for someone who'd never experienced the wonders of life beneath the sea, it was truly an amazing experience. Sea creatures, whether fish or crustaceans, were at our fingertips.

We had been told that the reef, just a few miles from shore, held even more beauty. The reef, being coral that rose from the floor of the ocean, allowed all of nature's vulnerable creatures in the seas to hide from those that preyed upon them. Those too bright and too small to hide in the open seas could blend into the colors and protection of the reef's coral.

We might have been young and in good physical condition, but a few miles from shore was a whole lot more than any of us were willing, or probably able, to swim.

We had a housekeeper named Elsie, and she was responsible for making sure our rooms were kept clean. She stressed that if we needed anything to let her know. Elsie was a beautiful person, maybe in her sixties, who was our "connection" to what any twenty-year-old wanted—and that would be the local produce.

Jamaica was learning that its beauty was a commodity, and the locals were finding their way in that trade. Tourism was still, to some degree, in its infancy.

Elsie was no different. She told us of a local guide that could take us out to the reef. We were told that he had an excellent reputation and a meeting was set up for his services the very next day. I guess he just happened to have a space open in his schedule. The next morning we met our guide at the beach. His name was Sam and his boat was state of the art, or maybe it would have been in 1950. The motor was much newer, probably from 1958.

He stood proudly by his boat, with a smile that any dentist would be proud of. We were not meeting at any yacht club with a boarding facility. The boat had been pulled up on the beach. There were no docks that his tour boat was pulled alongside of.

Sam asked our help in pushing the boat off the shore and into the sea and helped us climb aboard once the motor had cleared the land.

The motor probably used as much oil as it did gas, and I'm sure between the smoke from the engine and the smoke we exhaled from the local produce we could be easily followed by anyone watching from the shore.

We arrived at our destination, the reef. We all jumped overboard to explore the beauty beneath.

And beautiful it was. The coral and the fish were so vibrant in their colors they seemed as if they were glowing. Some fish were so small that they would not be seen if they were not in such stark contrast in their colors against a background of coral with differing colors.

The coral could be as bright as embers of coal glowing or on fire: red, orange, yellow, green, blue, indigo, and violet—hues of the rainbow seen through the prism of water reflected by the sun.

Or perhaps I was just stoned.

Tiring, I made my way back to the boat, and for the first time I noticed the boat's name written upon its side: LuV I sAm.

It was hand-painted, almost as if by a child first learning the alphabet and how to write.

Sam extended a hand and helped me climb aboard. There were no ladders or platforms to assist those wishing to get back onboard this luxury liner.

I sat with Sam while waiting for the others to return. The whole while we sat there, Sam used a coffee can to scoop water from the bottom of the boat back into the sea. Water was steadily finding its way into the boat through more than a few holes, and Sam was doing his best to keep the sea at bay.

I looked at Sam and made a little small talk. "Sam, it seems as though your yacht has a few leaks."

"Ya mon" was his only response. "Ya mon" was their English term for yes.

"Sam, just what does the name on the side of your boat mean?—Luv I Sam."

He looked at me with his ever-present smile and an expression of someone surprised at my asking a question with an answer that he thought should have been so obvious. His English was broken, a heavy island accent, though it was much better than the Jamaican I spoke, which was comprised of only "ya mon."

His response was the perfect explanation: "I Sam, everybody love I, so boat name, Luv I Sam."

Oh stupid me, how could I have not known?

The following year, some of my friends went back to Jamaica and they reported that "Luv I Sam" was still going to the reef, though the water was pouring in a little faster. Sam and his coffee can were bailing faster as well, keeping his vessel afloat and those that were along for the ride entertained.

And that ladies and gentlemen, boys and girls, in a nutshell is the same name as another person I came to know many years later.

The first Sam, the one Jamaica, I met in the early eighties. The second Sam, Sam Catalano, was thirty years later, and anyone fortunate enough to spend any length of time with him loved the guy.

His old boat was from the forties, and that old boat would be the vessel that carried him through life: his body. This Sam's vessel had a few leaks as well. His were caused by

Huntington's disease, and he kept his seas at bay with his own coffee can, his mind. His focus and determination kept the sea from sinking his vessel.

I'd had a feeling that both Sams would eventually succumb to their seas, and their vessels would be reclaimed by Mother Nature. The Sam in Jamaica had probably taken his last voyage on that old boat as the seas claimed what was theirs and he could not bail the water out fast enough.

My friend Sam would eventually lose his battle as well, as the seas of Huntington's poured in ever faster and his will no longer was able to keep that sea at bay. Even knowing the road that lay ahead of him, he displayed a character and a dignity that I will probably never again experience in this life.

In spite of his disease, or perhaps because of it, he enjoyed every day of his life. He took the time to listen to the people he came into contact with and loved all that his life had to offer.

Sam Catalano and I crossed paths because we both were social and enjoyed camping. I was fortunate enough to spend a little time with him. There are very few people in my life I've met that I will proclaim to others that they are a good person. To me it's a statement of their character and a testament to my word.

Sam is a good man.

This is the story of a few days I spent with a man I came to admire.

Chapter 2

The Irritant of Coral Becomes a Pearl

I had visited the Florida Keys in the past, the previous year having been my most recent, a little getaway from my day-to-day existence of workin' too much and playin' too little. Some fishing, the pleasure of others' company, and trying to turn a story that was in my mind and in a few notes into an actual book.

That year, while out on my boat upon the waters of the ocean, I had caught a fish and brought back into the campground. It soon became the talk for that day.

The campground was full of fishermen—and if I'm to be politically correct, fisherwomen (I hope this is the only time in these writings that I will be politically correct, so don't get used to it)—and any big fish that was brought to the cleaning station soon became fodder for conversation among those that fished, and that would be most any camper in the Keys, or within the confines of this campground.

The story told and retold was fun, what many a fisherman had experienced. Word of a big fish caught by someone in the campground gets around fast, and bragging rights last for all of a few minutes, maybe even a whole day. The next day would bring in another fish, another story, and bragging rights for someone else.

Many a fellow camper stopped by to see and photograph my catch and to hear the story surrounding it being caught. One camper in particular, a Mr. Charles Bailey, was the person who changed my perception of my own world.

The only thing he said was, "Dan, that's a wonderful story. You should write it down and send it to a magazine."

Chuck Bailey was a teacher, and his life was spent encouraging others to find their own potential or to explore their own possibilities. I think he found a worthy pupil in me.

I read, *so what the hell, I suppose I can write as well.* The next several days I was consumed with putting my experience into written words.

My story was published in three papers and suddenly I fashioned myself a writer, an author if you will. One paper even proclaimed me to be their "story of the month." And along with that honored title, I was presented with a rod and reel for my efforts.

It may have been only a local fishing paper, but to me it opened a whole new world. After all, not only had I been published, but I had been paid dearly for my efforts.

Ah yes, behold the author.

Mr. Bailey, with just a few words, changed my life and left me again dreaming of my future: a book completed. I was just a working fool, and my dreams had faded with age. The "what if" of a life perceived was again in my mind. The future with all its potential lay before me. It was mine for the taking.

I was young again.

Anyways, the thought of writing a story was something totally beyond anything that I had ever thought of, let alone attempted. Creativity was something I'd never experienced. I do enjoy songs and books, paintings, to some degree, though before writing a story, it was something far beyond anything I could ever truly comprehend.

Being creative starts with a thought that turns into something others might appreciate, whether it is visual or through words, to turn one's own feelings into something for others to talk about and critique, for better or worse.

What a concept!

To turn a thought into something others feel.

Creativity.

I had discovered it while vacationing the previous year, though it left me as quickly as it had found me upon returning home. A book that was all but writing itself suddenly found its way into the trash as soon as I left the borders of Florida.

From New York to the Keys of Florida, one thousand six hundred and twenty miles of road behind, I was crossing the final bridge leading back to that place where the previous year I had found something inside me that I was hoping was still there.

I was more than a little excited upon reaching that final bridge. Below that bridge was the ocean that I would soon be on with my boat. Below and to the left was the campground that awaited me. There was a sign at the end of that span: Big Pine Key Fishing Lodge.

I scanned the campsites along the shore, hoping to see the trailer of one camper in particular, that of Mr. Samuel Catalano.

* * *

I'd met so many wonderful people the previous year that I was looking forward to getting to know a little better, but Sam was someone I had found more interesting than most.

His character, his intellect, his wit made conversing fun. I guess I should say that he was a wiseass, like me. He had a quick wit and a sincerity that I found enjoyable.

Sam had been camping here for the last eight years, and I did not see his camper where I thought it should have been. He had a site right alongside the ocean, though I suppose that I was not really all that surprised.

I was disappointed, yes, but I guessed his days of camping were over. The reason I thought this? Well, let me explain.

As I said, I'd written an article that had found its way into a few papers. My article was even published in a local paper that came to the campground every week, and Sam, who was a fellow camper, had inquired about it.

"Dan, the talk around the campground is that you had a story in the local fishing paper, and I would love to read it. I had an article published before in a hunting magazine, and I'd really love to see what you wrote."

How could I not like the guy? He wanted to read my article.

"Sam, there is nothing I'd like more than to share it with you. Although I don't have my copy with me, I'll see if I can find it and bring it by your place later."

"I just want to read it. I'll give it right back. I'm sure you have family and friends that would like to see it as well."

Sam stressed his concern with his giving it right back. If I wasn't laughing outright, I'm sure I was at least smiling. The reason I found it amusing is because the paper that it was in was delivered to newspaper stands throughout the Keys, and it was free for the taking. In my excitement of having my story in print, I was so thrilled that I ransacked every newspaper stand between Key Largo and Key West, probably a hundred plus miles each way.

I started out taking just a paper or two, but by the end of my run, I was taking every one I could get my hands on.

I think I wound up with a hundred plus papers. In my delirium of being published, I actually thought they might be worth something someday.

Later that day I stopped by Sam's place with a copy, handed it over to him, and sat there while he read. I found myself eagerly awaiting his thoughts.

I had never really written anything other than a few love letters a lot of years before, and to have written something that some papers printed was exciting. To have someone want to read it was almost too much.

Here is my article, "A Shark's Tale from the Florida Keys."

* * *

I own and operate Daniel's Tree Service in the town of Gates, a suburb of Rochester, New York, though lately I have to wonder if it owns and operates me. This winter I decided to take a break.

To anyone that doesn't really know me, this may just be another fish story. To me it has already become a memory that I will forever cherish.

I woke up on Super Bowl Sunday excited, not because of the game, but because I was going fishing in the Florida Keys.

I started out fishing under the old Bahia Honda Bridge, an old abandoned railroad trestle. However, in a sixteen-foot boat with a strong wind and the tide moving at full speed, not to mention the warning signs saying "Watch For Falling Debris," I thought it best to move to another spot.

A little ways into the Atlantic Ocean, and a few yellowtail snappers later, I thought all was well. That is until the sharks decided to move in for an easy meal. It seemed as though every time I had a fish on the line, I couldn't bring it to the boat. The most I would bring in was either a mangled fish or just the head of one; more often than not, when I hooked something and began to retrieve it, my line would feel a heavy tug as the line would disappear from the reel before it was broken off.

I figured that the chum bag hanging over the side (a net-type bag that holds ground-up fish remains) wasn't helping, so I pulled it into the boat and again moved a short ways to another spot.

By then the tide had slowed and I decided to try casting from the front of my boat and working my bait slowly back. I had a fish on, and as I brought it out of the water and into my boat, a shark rose out of the depths with its jaws open, following its meal out of the water and into my face.

It was a bull shark, and all I saw was a mouth the size of a garbage can full of teeth rising at my feet.

Suddenly I wasn't so excited about ocean fishing. I put down my pole and got off the bow, or the deck, or whatever the hell you call the front of the boat, and sat down on the floor in the middle of my boat and began to question my priorities. I no longer was in love with the ocean and thought that maybe ice fishing was almost warming. Twelve inches of ice, with three layers of clothes on, in twenty-degree weather while trying to catch a twelve-inch yellow perch seemed rather appealing, almost comforting.

Thankfully (after a rather long discussion with myself), I decided to give it another try. I stood up and gradually found the courage to look over the sides of my boat. My newfound acquaintance didn't seem to be circling.

I again cast my bait into the seas and was rewarded with a fish that was doing its best to test both me and my tackle. It began to take line from my reel, though it didn't "feel" the same as the sharks had. When it jumped out of the water, even though it was long and narrow, I knew it was something different.

Fifteen minutes, or maybe an hour, later (time was not relevant; I really have no idea) and the fish was close to my boat. I have no idea how many times I had to put my pole in the water to keep him from tangling around the motor or anchor line as it circled my boat.

Ten feet from my boat, as he was beginning to tire, I thought the fight over, that is until a six-foot shark was closing in, followed by a hammerhead that was as long as my boat, which was sixteen feet, and the battle was really on!

The shark that rose at my feet scared me, really scared me, though these sharks had given me some warning and they wanted my fish, I wasn't about to give up.

I began to jump up and down on my boat, kicking the side as well as yelling, hoping to distract the sharks while still fighting the fish. I had to be a sight to behold.

My antics in dissuading those sharks left the fish on my line able to wrap around my motor and I broke my pole, a twenty-dollar flea market special just bought and talked down from twenty-five dollars (thank you very much).

I thought I had lost until I looked over the back of my boat and saw the tail of that fish extending past. I grabbed my gaff and brought him into the boat.

After a little hootin' and hollerin', I got out my fancy fishing index picture book and discovered that I had caught a Cobia.

I've been told that a Cobia once in a boat fights even harder than when in the water. I don't know if he was just plain ole tired or happy to be away from those sharks. I do know he didn't move.

I really have no idea if that Hammerhead was the length of my boat. He was probably bigger!

I may never be able to top this story, though I do know that it won't stop me from trying.

That Cobia wasn't the only one that was hooked that day. I was too.

Life can be truly wonderful, and today I think I will go back to that flea market and try to get back my money from that pole I bought that broke. I think I will buy something bigger and stronger.

After all, there is a Hammerhead out there that sure would make for an even better story.

* * *

Sam read and he would occasionally laugh, and all the while I watched and wondered about his thoughts on my writing.

Finally, he looked up. "Dan, this is really wonderful!"

Ah yes. The critics have approved! This was way too cool, writing something that others actually liked.

"Was that shark really sixteen feet?"

"No, Sam, I really think it was a whole lot bigger, though no one would have believed me, including you."

The previous year my sister and I had gone over to Bahia Honda State Park, and a ranger there had told us of a Hammerhead that swam these waters that was twenty-five feet long. (I couldn't think of a reason why he would say that to a tourist.)

After my experience, I went on the Internet and looked it up, and I found that people had seen a shark that big. They nicknamed him "Old Mo." Maybe they were exaggerating, maybe I saw his baby boy. I only know that I will never swim in the ocean again.

We sat together and basically got to know each other a little. Sam inquired about me and I asked about him.

"Dan, are you married?"

"No, I'm not, but I tried it once or twice."

Sam had been married, though only once.

"How about children, do you have any?"

"No, I never had the pleasure. It just didn't seem to work out that way, and how about you?"

"No. No children, Dan, I'm too selfish to have any kids. I love my own life too much. I wanted to do the things that I wanted to do, and with children I wouldn't have been able to do that."

I thought about that for a second and his very statement let me know Sam was a good person.

"Sam, I think you're full of shit. If you were selfish, you would have had kids and still done what you wanted. There are people out there with kids that do their own thing. They're the ones who are selfish."

He asked if I had any brothers or sisters.

"Actually, I am the seventh child of a seventh child."

Sam chimed in, "And the moon was in the seventh house?"

"Yes, and Jupiter was aligned with Mars, the seven moons of Saturn were at their closest point to the earth, and with my birth began the dawn of Dankind."

We both laughed and I continued, "I have four sisters and a brother, and I am the baby of the whole bunch."

"That would make you a sixth child."

"I had a sister that died," I said.

He wanted to know about the girl he'd seen me with the previous year, wondering if she was going to be my next wife, and I told her her name was Shawni and she was a friend who had just come down here for a little while.

We spoke for a while longer and I continued on my way.

I liked Sam. He seemed down to earth... and even more importantly, he said that he had enjoyed my article.

The next time I saw him, I was coming out of the front store/office. He was sitting in his vehicle. His eyes were welled with tears and he was rubbing them. I could only assume that after having read my article he was humbled by my very presence. I had to think that the article he had written paled in comparison to mine.

I stopped by his open window. "Sam, are you okay?"

"Hey, Dan, actually I'm not okay. I've got something in my eye and I can't get it out. It's probably just some sand or coral, but it's really bothering me."

A piece of anything in the eye is much more than just an irritant. It can be downright painful, and a piece of coral scratches the cornea to the point that even a grown man is brought to tears.

Oh well, so much for my thoughts of him being humbled by my writings.

"Sam, there's a drinking fountain around the corner. Why don't we go over there and try to flush it out?"

I helped him out of his car and we worked our way over. He was all but blinded by the irritant. Sam had some type of affliction that caused him to move around a whole lot more than most. His head would bob down then snap back, and his arms and legs were kind of herky-jerky in their movement.

I looked at the fountain, then at Sam, wondering if this was such a great idea. I told him to turn on the stream of water while I held his eye open and tried to keep his head from smashing into the metal spigot, all the while hoping to flush out the object of his discomfort. Many of Sam's movements seemed to be involuntary, making the job more difficult, and I wasn't sure if I was even doing any good.

"Sam, I do believe this ain't gonna work. Why don't you lie down on the bench and I'll go into the store and get a bottle of water and we'll try flushing it out?"

"Thanks, Dan. Put it on my tab."

Campers had accounts at the store, and Sam did not want me to pay.

I went to the counter with two bottles of water and put it on my account. I came back, water bottle in hand, to a Sam lying on his back on the bench. Looking at him lying there, I thought of a psychiatrist with his patient lying upon a couch. How could I possibly resist?

"Sam, you are my first patient, though let me assure you I do have some life experiences that may help me in helping you with whatever problems bring you here—if I may share a story of my niece's husband who *is* a psychiatrist, and his first patient. It seems a man came to him totally naked other than being wrapped in cellophane, and Dr. Mur said to this person, 'I can clearly see your nuts. Put on some underwear!'"

"So, Mr. Catalano, what brings you here to me? Perhaps you should tell me of your earliest childhood memories, and let me assure you anything and everything you tell me will be held in the utmost of confidentiality."

Sam just lay there in obvious discomfort, not even so much as a smile and I quit joking around and proceeded to flush his eye out. I went through both bottles of water, and whether or not successful, we didn't know. Sam was still in pain. An object in the eye even when gone can leave pain behind.

Brenda came out of the store and looked at the two of us, wondering what was going on. She was the person in charge of this establishment, the daughter to the matriarch who started it all, Joann. Sam told her that everything was okay, just a piece of coral in his eye and he thought that it had already been flushed out.

Brenda looked at the two of us. "Bullshit. You stay right there." She went back inside and in minutes returned. "Sam, I have an eye doctor waiting for us. Get in my car."

It wasn't a matter of whether or not he thought he needed to go to a doctor, it was stated as a simple fact that he was going.

I asked Brenda where the doctor's office was and said that I would take him. She barely acknowledged me.

Brenda looked at Sam. "Let's go. They are waiting for us."

I was impressed, and it gave me a little insight into the hierarchy of the campground, both of the establishment and those that had become regular guests, or rather those that were respected by that establishment.

Sam, it seemed, was an esteemed client. He had been coming here for a long time and everyone in the campground spoke highly of him, as did those who ran the place.

My final night of camping, before heading home, I decided to attend one of the many parties held at the campground. This one was hosted by the owner, Joann, outside her residence, which was just on the perimeter of the campground.

In actuality, it was the one and only party I had decided to attend.

It was a chance to say goodbye to those I had met and enjoyed during my stay. I noticed Sam standing behind a table where food was being served. As I approached him, he turned and started heading into the house behind him.

I called out to him, "Hey, Sam."

"DANNY! I need to check on the food inside. Come on in."

I followed him inside and I was in awe of the room we entered. Before me was a built-in pool within the house, and alongside the door we had just entered was a row of commercial stoves and ovens cooking or heating the food for the campers.

"What is this room?" I asked him.

"It's Joann's house."

Sam stood over a stove checking on some rolls that were heating. "Sometimes Joann lets me heat up her buns."

I looked around and let Sam know that I was not comfortable being in the owner's home without her telling me to enter. Even with his assurance that it was just the cooking area and everything was all right, I still did not feel right.

"I just wanted to say goodbye," I said. "I'll be leaving in the morning. I think I'll be heading back outside."

Shortly after, Sam came back out and headed over to me, asking if I'd be back the next year.

"I'm planning on it, and how about yourself?"

"I will be here as well."

The band was playing and Sam's body was bobbing and weaving, although it had nothing to do with the music.

I took the opportunity to mess with him a little bit. "You know, Sam, the way you always move about, it seems as though you don't need music to dance. You're always in motion. You must have women standing in line trying to keep up."

I'd never asked Sam what his affliction was. "Dan, I have Huntington's disease."

I looked at him and tried to show surprise. "Really, Sam? You have a disease? I guess I never noticed. I just assumed your staggering about was because you were drunk all the time."

Sam laughed. "It is the reason I move about so much. I've had it for seventeen years, and the doctors tell me that I've had it longer that anyone they know of, or at least longer than anyone still functioning."

And there it was. Sam stated it as a matter of fact, not looking for any kind of sympathy, merely explaining.

"What about medicine?"

He said that he was on medicine and it did help, although there was no cure yet.

We had spoken a while longer and had said our goodbyes.

* * *

And that, folks, is the reason I was looking for Sam's site in particular *this* year, but as I said, I guess I wasn't totally surprised that his camper was no longer there. I assumed his disease had progressed to the point where it was too difficult for him to return. Though disappointed, Sam was not the reason I was returning.

I was back to relax and fish, have some fun with new acquaintances and continue my foray into the world of writing.

Chapter 3

What a Wonderful World

Being self-employed, for nine months of the year I work my fanny off. It's pretty much all I do and it's okay by me. When I've been asked why I work so much, my response is the only answer that I can come up that makes any sense, at least to me: "It's just what I do."

I work... because I do. There really is no other reason, not for money. That's just a byproduct. Work is something I have always done and probably will do till the day I die. I am okay with that. I like working.

Once winter approaches and my work starts to slow—once the snow begins to fall—I put on my wings and head south. I'm a snowbird. That's a term the people that live in the South call those from the North who come down for the winter. I go south for the winter.

People down South seem to think "snowbird" is an insult. I don't. I spend the money I work hard for on a few months of fun. I gladly spend my money, and they gladly accept it.

I wear my wings proudly. I love where I'm from and I love where I migrate to. New York State has all four seasons, and each one of them is truly special, though our winter season goes on a bit too long and some years can seem to last for six months.

The calendar may say that the first day of winter is the twenty-first of December, but let me assure you that bleak weather for us usually arrives much earlier. Cold weather, gray skies, and snow come as early as October. By January many a person is already cranky and beginning to experience cabin fever, a disease caused by lack of sunshine, a lack of activity, and a lack of any kind of a life, other than their job, outside their home.

Those who do remain indoors cannot deny the beauty of nature after a snowfall if they're willing to look away from their television and out their windows. Every branch on a tree can hold several inches of snow, as does every bush and the ground beneath. If the sun is shining, it's a reflection on the landscape that creates a beauty that can be blinding.

To those willing to venture outdoors, they can find a winter wonderland: downhill skiing for those looking for thrills, or cross-country skiing for those who appreciate nature exposed and not hidden by foliage. Branches and shrubs devoid of leaves on a background of white expose the wildlife that normally is hidden. An incline or a decline, no matter how small, becomes a hill filled with the squeals of children as they first discover sledding.

Children, as well as those adults who refuse to grow up, those who still believe in Santa Claus, can hear sleigh bells on the eve before Christmas and maybe see the tracks of reindeer left in the snow. A white Christmas lives not only in songs but in memories as well.

A snowflake accumulates with others and turns into snow on the ground, and those flakes rolled into others turn into a snowball, and that snowball with a few rolls over the other snowflakes suddenly becomes a snowman.

Winter can be beautiful, though much of nature goes dormant or heads for warmer weather, and it makes spring that much more special.

The arrival of spring brings everything to life, both for Nature and those that hibernate in their homes. Trees begin to bud as the landscape becomes alive and changes from gray to green.

Songbirds return and waste no time in letting it be known that they are horny and looking for love. They puff out their chests while strutting about, their pickup lines through their songs. I guess it's kind of like the youth of today without the benefit of song, although they are almost as entertaining to watch.

The sun not only warms the land, it warms the hearts of people. Those who were grumpy suddenly find themselves smiling with no provocation from others.

Spring in New York is my favorite time of the year. I so enjoy being awakened long before the sunrise by those birds with their boisterous songs, looking for love.

They say it's the early bird that gets the worm. I think it's more likely that the early bird is hoping to share his "worm."

Farmers turn the soil and plant their seeds. The buds of the trees turn into leaves, and flowers adorn the landscape with petals of red, pink, orange, and so many colors that to drive along a street with flowering trees is to experience such a beautiful display of nature. It's sad that many people never see that beauty, let alone appreciate it. They drive to wherever they are in a hurry to get to, never truly appreciating the beauty that is so bountiful right outside their window. Even sadder yet is the new generation that has their noses buried so deeply in the latest electronic gadget that the only thing they see is someone else's pictures or thoughts, and they are only too ready to share that rather than their own thoughts or what they see.

Every city, every town, has it, and unless it is promoted, it is lost on the masses. Washington, D.C., has its cherry blossoms, Rochester, New York, has the lilac festival, North Carolina celebrates its azaleas, and I'm sure most cities and towns have something they would love to show to the world.

Many people see New Year's Day as a new beginning. For me, spring is when life begins anew. Spring turns into summer, buds turn into leaves, and blossoms come into fruition.

Gardens planted with seed begin to push upward through the earth as they find the sun and the smell of air and raindrops upon them. People expose a bit more flesh as temperatures rise, and that's not always a pretty thing.

As summer progresses, nature "bares" the first of her fruits: strawberries, blueberries, and various vegetables. I enjoy produce from a store, though there is no comparison to that grown by your very own self.

Whether it is the anticipation or the actual taste, I don't know, but wiping the dirt off a tomato and biting into its flesh can't be bought.

Autumn reaps the harvest of the rest of those seeds that were planted in the spring. Pumpkins and cornstalks adorn the landscape. Cider bought from a store will never compare to the taste of that from a farmer's stand.

I suppose that's not true. Sooner or later farmers will have to conform to the same regulations that give big business' products a long shelf life. (The powers that be are more inclined to listen to those who line their pockets than to the voice of the peons just trying to make a living.) I guess small farmers and those who buy from them do not have a loud enough voice to be of any worth to those who claim to represent us.

As autumn progresses and its produce is harvested, Mother Nature begins to go into hibernation. She shuts off the flow of life to her leaves, and it is displayed in a beauty that neither artist with paints and canvas nor any photographer with a camera can truly capture.

Though beauty is seen through the eyes, it is only through the soul that it is felt and appreciated. It's the same with a song, a poem, or anything in life for that matter. What is beautiful to one person will never be quite the same to another. Beauty is felt within. The eyes, the ears, the smell are merely conduits to the heart.

Those of the world who critique others' work only express their own feelings or interpretations, and it's unfortunate that they dictate to the masses not able or willing to think for themselves.

I suppose that those who can't be successful in their art either critique, or, if they love their craft, they help others and teach. Any art, any beauty, felt by one person will not be denied to the spirit of that person as long as he ignores the voices of others.

Leaves turn from green to every color that Crayola tries to recreate. Reds range in color from scarlet to a dull rust, yellows from the brightness of the sun rising on the water to the orange of its sunset reflected upon the dust of a desert. Pinks, purples, brown everything between.

"Roy G. Biv," (the old memory device for the colors of the rainbow), ain't got nuthin' on a New York autumn. It is a display that, while driving along the hills and valleys of the Finger Lakes mirrored in the waters, I will never be able to truly recreate through my words.

As autumn turns to winter, leaves fall from the trees, blanketing the ground beneath. Trees devoid of leaves become mere skeletons exposing the gray of their bark beneath, a reflection of the gray clouds above.

Winter in New York.

One thousand and six hundred plus miles to the south it's still winter, at least by the standards of those who live there year-round.

To those of us only visiting, it's paradise. Long underwear is replaced by shorts; a hat that warms the ears becomes a hat that shades from the sun. Clothing is replaced by sunscreen.

I left New York on a Friday morning, and by Saturday afternoon I had gone from my truck's heater to its air conditioner.

For whatever reason, when I am traveling I just cannot sleep. An hour in a rest stop results in a ten-minute nap. I am restless while traveling. A friend once told me that I should slow down, that I should take my time to smell the roses.

My response, "Fuck a bunch of roses. I grow roses and smell them back home. I'm going fishing."

Arriving at my destination, I checked in at the front office and received my pass into the campground.

My home for the duration of my stay was a camper that sits on the back of my pickup truck. It extends over the cab and is called a "slide in." Towed behind that contraption was my boat, and they were both filled with everything and anything that would make my stay more comfortable.

I backed both boat and truck into my campsite, disconnected the boat, and parked my truck. I was more than a little tired and the only unpacking I did was to clear a few things on the floor of my camper that made it easier to get into, those few things and a six pack. I was on vacation after all.

A few people stopped by with hugs and their salutations of "welcome back."

Miss Helen and Mr. Lou were still at their campsite directly across from me, and I was oh so glad for that. The previous year Lou had become what I considered not only a friend but my mentor of the high seas.

Both fishing spots and those tricks used to catch the fish beneath are highly guarded by those who've taken the time required to learn them, and until you've proven yourself worthy, they are rarely shared.

For whatever reason, Lou took me under his wing that first year. I don't know if it was that I amused him with my childish mannerisms, or because he saw a little bit of himself in me, or maybe he just felt sorry for me.

Lou was someone with whom I was hoping to reacquaint. He reminded me a lot of my father, a man of few words, though through his actions he spoke loudly. I was back, and Lou was again my neighbor.

It had been a long trip, and after a few beers and a few hugs, I found my way into my camper and my bed.

I was more than a little pooped. Sleep did not elude me and I slept deeply that night.

Chapter 4

First Day

The next morning I awoke to the most beautiful of sounds: the sounds of Nature.

My stay for my vacation was nothing fancy, a camper that kept me dry and, to some degree, out of the elements. When you are not insulated from the rest of the world by the walls and insulation of a house and the property in between, you become a bit more aware of your surroundings and you hear the sounds outside of yourself so much more so. In this case, I was being rewarded with birds singing, birds that were welcoming a new day, or perhaps they were welcoming me?

The cheaper your camper, the more you hear from the outside, and the more that others hear from inside yours. Someone in a tent farts, and two campsites away it is not only heard, it is sometimes felt, and if you happen to be walking by, you may even see a tent swell up a bit. Someone in a camper with hard sides might only be heard one campsite away.

Anyways, I awoke to the music of dear ole Mother Nature in a camper that let the sounds of the world in. In this case, the birds that were perched on the limbs that extended above and over my camper. They were singing their songs so loudly that I figured they must have missed me as much as I did them.

I lay there, doing nothing other than listening. It's such a simple thing to listen and enjoy the present, though it's something for whatever reason that I don't seem to do in my day-to-day life.

Maybe I had lain there too long and thought too much and began to think that possibly it wasn't a song expressing my welcome. Maybe those birds were just pissed at my being under their favorite tree.

I got out of bed and made a pot of coffee, or I guess it would be more appropriate to say that I turned on the stove that held the coffee pot that had been prepared the night before and was sitting upon the stove waiting to be brewed into my morning wake-up drink.

Perked coffee is something else I don't seem to take the time to make back home, even though it takes only a few extra minutes. It's such a simple pleasure that I always tell myself that, upon returning home, I'll at least make it on weekends, though of course I rarely ever do.

The smell and the sound of coffee perking, the aroma that permeates the room, is kind of like the smell of roses. It's another thing I tell myself that I need to take the time to appreciate when I return home that in actuality I won't.

I poured myself a cup of brew and sat outside enjoying my first taste and my surroundings and being alone with no distractions. The sun had yet to rise. The stars were fading as the sun crept closer to the horizon. Though the birds were awake, most of the campground was not, and I was at peace sitting at my table with my cup of coffee and no place to go and nothing to do.

A few cups of coffee later, with the caffeine working its way into my being, I began to think about what needed to be done that day when I realized I was doing just that.

Nothing!

Nothing is everything when your normal day-to-day schedule is getting to a job only to complete it so you can get on to the next job and complete that so you could get to the next. It's a sad cycle that I've allowed myself to get caught up into. It's pretty sad when you wish for more hours in a day so you can get more work done.

I do a lot for my customers, and they seem to be my main concern when back home, maybe my only concern. When I'm in the Keys, I have no responsibilities, no one who is looking for me to help them with the truly unimportant things in life.

Tree trimming or removal has no effect on the rest of the world. Luckily for me it matters to a lot of homeowners. Trees too close to a house can cause damage to roofs. Dead or broken limbs pose a hazard to those beneath. A property is enhanced by the beauty of a maintained landscape. That home benefits, and the property of the neighborhood does as well. I guess that in my world money does grow on trees.

Don't get me wrong, I do enjoy my work, and my customers do appreciate me and the job done by my employees. It's just that, after a while, the running around gets a little old. I think I have come to enjoy the interaction with my customers as the best part of my day, not so much the work being done. One job is basically the same as the last or the next, though people are always different and occasionally I'll find one who is unique (weird to some), and I like that.

I had a seventy-year-old woman one time that was showing off her shepherd and Rottweiler. When I told her that as I got older, I liked the little "foo foo" dogs, she took one look at me with disgust on her face and said, "I knew it. You ain't nothing but a fucking pussy!"

I burst out laughing.

How can you not love someone like that?

I was in the Florida Keys and doing absolutely positively nothing that mattered in the scheme of the universe, and two hours later I was still doing the same thing.

My campsite was in a section of the campground known as "Rustic," called that because it was without electricity or running water. It was a place for those who didn't mind not having cable TV or who could walk a little ways for their morning shower. It was for those who could keep their bowels in check till they made it to the bathroom.

My site was designated number one in the nonelectric section, or as it was also called among those with all the amenities of finer living (electricity and running water), the Primitive section. Those who reside in the electric section we in Nonelectric refer to as Tin City because of their houses on wheels with metal sides.

Personally I like to refer to those in Primitive as "those with social skills and barbeque grills" and those in Electric as "those with TV Guides and aluminum sides." Those in Electric even had running water and toilets that flushed!

Eventually, most in the nonelectric moved into Electric as they got older, though not all. It was a life style that some just... liked.

Those who were left behind referred to them as traitors for leaving the simple life for the easy life. They traded in their lanterns and solar panels for a light switch and a receptacle, the entertainment of their fellow campers for a television set.

I say those without electricity kept it simple, though I suppose those who resided in Electric kept it a whole lot easier: a remote control for their TV so they didn't have to get out of their La-Z-Boy recliner, a switch for a light that they didn't need fuel for, and a pot of coffee with a timer that was ready before they even opened their eyes instead of brewing coffee that had to be watched and waited for.

Their camper would be on one border of their site to maybe the halfway point, and an awning would stretch to the other border. The awning may have protected them from the sun and rain, but they missed out on the beauty of a starlit night. The awning and the lights they had hung to adorn their patio never allowed the stars to shine through. The heavens above were replaced by lights below that twinkled for all to say "look at me."

Some even adorned the palm trees with lights. Don't get me wrong. I truly love lights that hang from houses and the surrounding areas from Thanksgiving until January 1, though I just don't get it afterwards. At least most of those here turn off those displays when they go inside for the night (most).

There was even a section along the canal that was considered "prime" real estate, at least to those in the electric section. Some of those people called it the Riviera.

The rest of the campground called it Death Row.

It was rare that one of these sites became available. More often than not, it did only when one of the current occupants died.

Oh well, enough of that. Let's get back to my site.

Along the front of my campsite was a road, or more appropriately, a path, and across from that road was another row of campsites filled with my fellow campers.

The back of my site was an area that was designated "forever wild" and it stretched for quite some distance before it ended at the ocean. It was so designated because of the deer that depended on its habitat for their survival, their very existence. It was protected by the federal government and was a designated wilderness area.

Key deer only exist on a few of the islands within the Florida Keys. They are a subspecies of whitetail deer and their habitat is very limited. To not regulate this region would be to condemn their existence to a few zoos, or to a head mount trophy from days gone by.

They are a stunted version of the whitetail deer due to their habitat and limited food supply, and it was a land that could not be developed for the sake of those deer. Their safety was a reward to more than just those deer. It benefited all those who ever had the time or inclination to sit and appreciate "deer" ole Mother Nature.

Another benefit, at least for me, was the low area that held water that, depending on the rainfall, could almost reach the steps of my camper. It held small fish and wading birds searching for a meal, and every day I awoke to their being there: herons, ducks, egrets, and others that I couldn't identify, though their names didn't matter to me. They were beautiful to watch. Knowing their names is just an easy way to let others know what you saw.

Bird watchers have their checklist of birds they've seen. An ignorant fool like me couldn't tell the difference between a jay bird and a blue jay or a bluebird or even the Bluebird of Happiness that shits on my Cheerios in the morning.

There are times when I just enjoy the moment, the beauty of life around me, and I find myself experiencing it when in the Keys.

I sat outside savoring the aroma and the taste of my coffee. As it began working its way into me, the weariness of the road began to leave. After drinking my first pot of coffee, I thought that I should get off my lazy ass and do something.

After the second pot, my thoughts began to concentrate on what needed to be done that day.

Two hours later, I thought that maybe I should really unload my supplies and set up my campsite. Another hour later the only thing I had accomplished was a shower.

By the time the sun was setting, all I had accomplished was unloading my charcoal grill and a lounge chair. Hey, what can I tell ya folks? When in Rome...

I was in the Keys of Florida after all and I was doing absolutely positively nothing that really mattered, though in actuality whomsoever amongst us ever does anything that matters after a generation or two passes?

Who could possibly ask for nothing more?

In the Keys, the smell of the ocean (rotting sea weed, decaying fish that had washed upon the shore), the smell of shrimp boiling, the occasional smell of marijuana, as well as the smell of the old hippie smoking it, is as wonderful as any perfume created by man to hide the smell that emanates from all of us. (Old hippies really don't smell; they have come to the realization that it's cool to shower.) The women even seem to shave their armpits. (It's the Europeans and young hippies that still don't.)

The back of my campsite sometimes held stagnant water and its aromas also exuded the beauty of nature.

Fuck a bunch of roses. I have my campsite within the Keys and the odors that emanate from within and without. If "Paradise Lost" truly was, then I thought I'd found it, at least I had found mine. I could also be happy in knowing I was nowhere near the "dumping" station where campers emptied the holding tanks from their campers that contained their bodily waste, as well as anything else that went down the drain of their sink or toilet. It went into a tank beneath the ground, waiting to be pumped into a truck.

The bowels of people are evacuated into the campers that people stay in, and those are emptied into a tank beneath the earth, then into a tank on a truck, only to be transported to a place that would add a few ingredients and return them back into the bowels of the earth to enrich the soil for the produce that would feed those campers, only to be returned back in kind. (I think. I have no idea where the poop goes after leaving me.)

Before I knew it, the sun was gone and the light of day was fading, and being more than a little road weary, I retired into my camper with my notes from the year before that I anticipated would become a book, and I tried writing. It wasn't too long till I found my way to bed and sleep found me.

Chapter 5

Snow Bird #5

The next morning came, and though awake—my eyes being open was the reason I thought I was awake—I lay in bed almost as if glued there. My body wasn't ready to listen to my brain that was already up.

My normal day-to-day routine back home is to hit the ground running: a pot of coffee, a shower, and on to my first job of the day. Being in the Keys, with no place I had to be and nothing I had to do, I had no reason to get out of bed.

The feeling lasted but a few minutes. The excitement of having nothing to do left me not wanting to waste another minute of the day. I jumped out of my bed, turned on my stove, and after the few minutes it took my coffee grounds to come to fruition, I stepped outside with my cup in hand and sat at my picnic table, inhaling my surroundings.

All of my senses came to life in the Keys: seeing, smelling, and hearing everything that surrounded me. Even my toes felt the warmth or the coarseness of the earth beneath.

At the back of my campsite stretched an area quite some distance before reaching the ocean. It mainly consisted of mangrove trees, a tree that could be rooted in very little soil, and sometimes even into the ocean, their density so thick that they were all but impenetrable by man.

Birds were in the wading area in the back of my site, it being designated number one in Rustic. I was back in the land of those I considered my peers. Whether they considered me theirs only time would tell.

I like people, and campers for the most part were pretty much as real a people as there are.

Some that resided here had educations that included a BS, MS, or PhD (and I ain't got no idea what any of those mean). I just knew they were a bit more "edicated" than I is.

Retired teachers and lawyers slept next to the weekend derelicts or the unemployed who collected a check from the government. They ranged from those who busted their fannies making a paycheck to those who had done quite well in life and just enjoyed being among others. (Either that or they were cheap bastards not willing to spend their fortunes.) I suppose I fell somewhere in between, but I was not sure which end of the spectrum I was closer to.

Campers are pretty much down-to-earth, and for the most part (at least in this place, in Rustic) are not out to impress so much as they are to have fun, a community of people who enjoy other people and keep their lives kinda simple. It was a wonderful feeling having no one dependent on my presence. Being lazy was not part of my makeup, and that made it even better, if only for today.

I looked over my writings of the previous night and had no idea what I was trying to say. Birds waded in the area in front of me and sang above and around me, native birds and those that migrated here for the winter.

A few cups of coffee and a bowl of oatmeal later and it was time to get off my fanny. I'd had a day to recoup from my trip here and that was enough. I probably should set up my campsite, my home for the duration of my stay. My boat, as well as my camper, was loaded with anything and everything I thought I'd need. I backed my truck into the spot where I wanted my camper and unloaded chairs, a propane stove, a Weber charcoal grill, fishing gear, coolers, all the amenities to make my life simple for my stay. My home was complete.

My boat, still in my campsite, really needed to be in the ocean. I backed my pickup to the boat's trailer, hooked them together, and drove upfront to the boat launch.

I was more than a little excited as I backed the trailer into the water and watched the boat float off it and into the ocean.

My slip was no more than a few feet from the boat launch and a rope tossed to someone there waiting to help me was enough to put my boat in its spot. I didn't know the person, though most people willingly lent a hand to others.

I expressed my gratitude and pulled my trailer out of the water and found a place to park it for the next month. I returned my truck to my campsite and walked back to my boat. It hadn't been in any water since my last time here, almost a year ago.

I was excited, no, *ecstatic*. Something about the ocean makes me feel young again. Whether it be my childhood relived or just childlike behavior being free with no boundaries, I don't know. I do know that it's as fun as anything I do.

Climbing into my boat and casting its ties from its moor, I started the engine and left the sanctity of land for the solace of the sea. I cleared the channel that led into the ocean before pushing the throttle all the way forward and left Big Pine Key behind.

I slowed to guide my boat under the bridge that led into Florida Bay, then turned back along the shore of another Key, and after a little ways came upon the Bahia Honda channel and another bridge that spanned that distance.

I went under it and back into the ocean and again pushed the throttle forward, going maybe a mile out. My boat was small, only sixteen feet, and the seas were more than a little rough. In a small boat at thirty-plus miles an hour in rough seas, I found myself airborne several times. Sometimes even the propeller of my motor would scream as if demanding to be put back into the sea. The salt of the ocean burned my eyes and its spray stung my flesh.

I was again reborn and I didn't need to be dunked into water that was anointed by the Holy Spirit. I think that my parents and my God done good the first time.

No sunscreen, no hat, and I do believe that this fair-skinned white boy would probably wind up with more than a little color.

Oh the travesty of being in the sun and on the ocean. It's a tough life in the tropics, but with a little bit of time I would learn to get used to it.

I turned my boat parallel to the other side of the first Key I had gone along and headed back toward camp. The trip had been no more than a few miles or so, yet water was dripping from every part of me. As I pulled my boat back into its slip, I'm sure my smile was as blinding as the Florida sun reflecting off the water.

I looked to the heavens above. "Thank ya, Lord, thank ya, Jesus. I am back!"

Leaving my boat, I headed back to my campsite and was interrupted by people with hugs and salutations of "welcome back."

I sat at my picnic table with a beer, content with my lot in life. I may not have much money in the bank, but I have my paradise, if only for a little while in the winter. I had no idea of the time of day, probably late afternoon, but I didn't care. Upon crossing that final bridge on the drive here to my campsite, time was no longer that important.

I contemplated getting out my notes, though before I could do anything, a few people began to stop by. They figured I'd had a day to rest and that was enough.

Actually, more than a *few* people stopped by with more than a few beers, and after a lot of a few more people and a lot of a few more beers, I found my way into my camper and my bed.

It sure was nice being back.

Chapter 6

Coffee With Sam

In the recesses of my mind, I heard the chirps of birds. Sleep and the subconscious were slowly replaced by the semiconscious and awareness of my surroundings, which became the real world around me. And oh what a beautiful world it was.

I'd not heard birds and their songs in quite some time. The expressive ones had left New York before the cold had arrived, and it seemed as though they and those native to Florida were quite happy with their lot in life, a lot like some of the campers—loud and letting everything and everyone know that they were happy to be here.

As I lay there, thoughts of my day's schedule of things to do replaced any remaining thoughts of sleep. I jumped out of bed, turned on the pot of coffee, and stepped outside before I realized that some pants might be a good idea.

I put on a pair of shorts and a shirt, then went back out. Campers are tolerant for the most part, though the vision of my lily-white ass would probably be more than they would or could tolerate. I didn't want anyone to think there was still a full moon out.

It was not even six. The sun had yet to rise and the front store had yet to open. Once the store opened, coffee was free for the taking to all those within the confines of the campground, and that was still a couple hours away.

The previous year, my ritual had been a cup or two of my own coffee, if not the whole pot, before going up front to enjoy the companionship and stories of my fellow campers. It was good coffee; it was wonderful people; and the conversation was at least entertaining. Free coffee and free advice. Well, at least the coffee was worth the price of admission, and the conversation...? I guess you get what you pay for.

After a few cups of my own coffee at my own picnic table, I decided to head to the showers to clean up. While ascending the stairs, I heard a familiar voice exchanging conversation with others below me and turned around.

Lo and behold, right there below the showers and a row of campers and a road separating his campsite from mine was Sam. I yelled out, probably too loud for this time of the day (a lot of people were still sleeping). "Sammy!"

Sam looked up at me, smiled, and responded, also a bit too loud for this time of day, "DANNY, you're back!"

"I most certainly am, Sam."

"Give me a few minutes. I need a shower and a poop. I'll be back in a few."

Shit, showered, and shaved, I headed back to Sam's site. He was sitting in a chair alongside his picnic table. He stood up and held out his hand, and I did as well. "Hi, Dan."

"Hey, Sam. You've moved campsites."

"Sorry, Dan. I hope you're not too awfully disappointed. The reason I moved was because I wanted to be closer to you."

I laughed and Sam said that the reason he had relocated was to be closer to the restrooms. The medication he was on left him more tired, and the energy he had he did not want to waste on walking the additional hundred yards or so to the showers or bathroom. It was just a little too far when you had to go.

"Dan, any chance you have coffee made? I don't make it myself anymore. I leave too big a mess. It's not worth the effort and the store isn't open yet."

"Hell yes. I've got a pot going every morning, and I still might have a little left."

I told him said to stay put. I went back to my campsite and I returned with two empty cups and a pot with a few cups left. I poured us both some.

"Sam, I'm glad you made it back, I was beginning to think that you hadn't."

"I am back, Dan, and you are too."

The previous year I had told him that, after discovering writing, I had a book in the works.

"How is your book coming along?"

"Not good, Sam. Last year I think it came to me almost too easily. A thought turned into written words without any help from me, and I've done absolutely nothing with it since—a few half-assed attempts with half-assed results. I'm hoping being back here I can do something with it. In the meantime, I guess I'll go fishing. So how are you? How are you doing? You seem about the same as last year."

"I'm *good.*"

He emphasized the word "good," and the more I got to know him, the more I realized that he sometimes made sure his feelings were known by almost shouting certain words. It was a part of his disease that he was no longer in control of, something even as simple as his voice inflection. He was losing control of his speech.

While we were sitting there, another camper stopped and Sam introduced us. "Dan, this is Jim from Michigan."

"Hi, Jim from Michigan, I'm Dan from New York."

It was a common theme among those here, or I suppose those that vacation anywhere, to say where you were from. We shook hands and exchanged pleasantries.

He told Jim to sit down and I held up the pot of coffee, offering him some.

Jim declined, saying that he'd already had enough for the day. "Sam, I just stopped by to bring you a breakfast sandwich from Mary. She cooked more than I could eat today."

Sam thanked Jim and told him to make sure he thanked his wife as well. "Jim, Mary is a wonderful woman. She really is lovely. The only thing that seems to be wrong with her is she must be a poor judge of character."

I laughed, and Jim just sat there, either ignoring the comment or not understanding.

Sam continued, "Hey, Jim, today is Tuesday. It's golf day, isn't it?"

Every Tuesday the campground has a league that plays at a local par-three golf course and Jim was a regular. "We do golf today, Sam, though let me assure you it's not as much fun as it used to be. For whatever reason, they now allow women to play, and they just seem to bring the game down. We now even have women in this league."

I was more than a little amused, though Jim was very serious in his comments. I had to come up with one of my dumb-assed comments. How could I not?

I asked Jim if he knew the difference between a golf ball and a "G" spot.

He raised his eyebrows and said, "A what?" He continued with his tirade. "When women play, all they really want to do is talk. Now that I think of it, that's all they ever really do."

I told Jim that the campground was having a female-only kayak trip coming up in a few days. They were calling it the Kayak yak yak yak trip. Jim thought that was so appropriate a name and laughed. I didn't have the heart to tell him that I was only kidding, that there was no such trip.

Jim continued with his rant on golf and the way women ruined what should be a man's time to be with other men. "They hit the ball maybe fifty yards, and they all have to walk together to one another's ball and they talk the whole time. They hit the ball, and they laugh, and they walk to the next woman's ball. You know, I really don't think they should even allow women to be on the course before one o'clock."

I couldn't resist. "Hey, Jim, I've heard rumors that they even started allowing them colored folk to play golf. Please say it ain't so Joe."

"My name's Jim."

"Sorry, Jim, what's next? Collard greens at the Masters?"

Jim continued on with his grumbling, never even acknowledging my comment. "God dammit, golf used to be fun. It used to be relaxing, for crying out loud. Well anyways, I'm off. I'll see you guys later."

Jim got up and started leaving, then stopped and turned around. "Dan, it was nice meeting you."

"Jim, let me assure you it really was my pleasure."

Jim told Sam that he was making chili later that day and he'd bring him a bowl by.

I looked at Sam. "You know, Jim seems like a nice enough fellow, though I really don't think he ever found golf very relaxing." I laughed and Sam smiled.

"He is a good person, Dan, but I think you're right. I do believe he is a little bit on the competitive side."

"Ya think? Maybe only just a little bit competitive?"

Sam asked me just what was that question I asked Jim about a golf ball and a "G" spot.

"My sister once asked me, 'What's the difference between a golf ball and a "G" spot?' I said that you could find a golf ball, and she responded that a guy will spend ten minutes looking for a golf ball. I thought it was funny."

Sam laughed.

"Sam, my sister said that every guy she told it to thought it was dumb, and I was the only one that found it funny. I guess you are the second."

We finished the coffee. I told Sam that I had been really looking forward to fishing and that by now the bait shop would be open in town.

"I gotta git going, Sam. There's some fish out there that are cold because of it being winter here, and I've a grill that will warm them up nicely."

"Good luck, Dan, and thank you for the coffee."

"Stop by tomorrow morning. I'll have a pot on the stove and will be expecting your company. I'm awake by six, and if I'm not outside just tell me to get my lazy ass up."

It was to become my morning ritual, my daily ritual of coffee with Sam.

Leaving him, I returned to my campsite and hopped into my truck and headed into town to buy some bait for a day of fishing.

I stopped at the same bait shop that I had gone to the previous year and was happy to see that Terry still worked there. She was a pleasure to buy bait from, upbeat and cocky at the same time.

Terry was a wee bonnie lass with a heavy Scottish brogue. She was also half daft and sometimes spoke loudly, thinking her voice was only a whisper. She could cuss like any sailor on shore leave after a few hours in a port bar. She was absolutely wonderful.

Anyways, she welcomed me back with a hug and we walked into the back where the shrimp were kept, leaving a customer at the front door who had already paid. When she asked me how many I wanted, I told her to give me four. She looked at me, and though she thought she was whispering, she was actually quite loud. (She had two hearing aids and didn't realize the volume of her voice.)

"YOU MEAN FOUR DOZEN?"

I replied that of course I meant four dozen.

She told me about the previous customer. "That fucking asshole that just left wanted four as well and when I put four dozen into his bucket he said that he only wanted four shrimp.

What kind of asshole goes fishing with only four fucking shrimp!"

Terry's "whisper" was loud enough that it could have been heard outside. Along with her accent, it was almost too much. I burst out laughing when I heard the front door slam as the customer she had sold the four shrimp to left.

I was back among good people and had an ocean full of fish that were sitting there anticipating a free meal from the rookie of the previous year.

I headed back to camp and packed my boat with food and water and my fishing gear. I cranked up the engine and headed out into the high seas.

Everyone has chains that bind them in life, and it's not necessarily a bad thing, though for whatever reason when I leave the land behind, I also leave behind my life as it was. There are ties that bind me, yet when I am experiencing the tides and winds, I am no longer bound. I think of everything in life or nothing at all.

"I am free, free at last." (Forgive me, Dr. King. The ocean is *my* freedom.) I am probably even misquoting here.

The sea is where I commune with my god, and it's peaceful, and the bounties of that god are sometimes given, sometimes not, and I accept that.

I returned to land with a few fish and a feeling of being quite content—a few fish for my supper cooked on my charcoal grill and I retired to my camper.

A full belly and an empty mind is a most wonderful thing, and I didn't want to waste it. Though I tried to fill my head with thoughts for my book, I just couldn't, and my bed looked like just the place for thinking.

Chapter 7

Another Way to Start My Day

Waking to the sounds of chirping birds is a wonderful way to start a day. It is so much more enjoyable than my normal routine of the morning news on the television, checking out the weather report for that day that was only a "maybe" and only in the background of my thoughts (because rarely did I let it influence my plans for that day). Weathermen are paid to tell us what might happen. I get paid to do something that others want done, and I drink my coffee while making a lunch for later that day.

A few campers tend to stay up later than they might otherwise back from wherever they came. They socialize and maybe have a cocktail or two, maybe even three or four or... What I do know is that nobody (at least in Rustic) counts those numbers.

Those in Rustic tend to socialize a little bit later, maybe even earlier, than those in Electric (I think.) There is no TV show that those in Electric have to get home to that will entertain them.

Some in Rustic might read books during the course of the day in the sunlight, and by night a gathering will usually be a part of their entertainment. They camp in this section because they enjoy the company of others, though most get up before the sun, and a few of them sit on the shore with coffee cups in hand awaiting its rising over the ocean and its reflection off the sea and the clouds above. Every morning, as the stars begin to fade and the birds test their vocals, a few campers move about.

I heard footsteps approaching my campsite, footsteps upon the coral. It's a distinctive sound when someone walks. The roads or pathways traveled within the confines of the campground are not made up of pavement or concrete.

Coral is the road of choice. Its availability makes it cost-effective, and it allows rainfall to drain and flow back into the sea. With being only a few feet above sea level, there is not a lot of soil to absorb the water. Rain is not only frequent, it sometimes can come down quite heavy in South Florida, and soil or dirt would be washed into the sea almost as soon as it was laid down.

Walking on those roads of crushed coral creates a noise as the feet push coral into coral, and with Sam's shuffling it was even more so.

"Oh, Danny, are you awake?"

Sam's voice was no more than a loud whisper. Space is limited within the confines of a campground; every foot wasted is money lost. Your camper is as little as ten feet from your neighbor's, and most people are respectful of others' space. Sam was probably even more so than most.

"I most certainly am, Sam," I said, "and have been barely able to sleep all night anticipating your arrival. Give me a minute. I'm still naked and would hate for you to think you were short-changed when they handed out the penises."

Clothed, I stepped outside with a pot of coffee that I had already brewed inside on my stove.

"Good morning, Dan. Is that offer for coffee still open?"

"Good morning, Sam. I meant it when I said it, and it will remain in effect for the duration of my stay."

I poured Sam a cup and set the pot down on the picnic table. A bird landed on that table and it immediately started to peck at the coffee pot, almost attacking it. Sam was amused and commented that the bird must not like its own reflection.

I looked at him and said, "Sam that pot has been on my table many a morning and no bird has ever bothered with it. It makes me wonder if it's your reflection that's bothering him and that coffee pot brings you down to his size." I didn't give Sam a chance to respond as I changed the subject. "Those birds over there, they're egrets?"

Before responding, Sam pointed out that the bird was actually on my side of the table, then he looked at those birds in back of my site, then at me and smiled. "Very good, Dan. Yes, they are indeed egrets and their taste is absolutely delicious. In fact, they taste just like eagle."

I laughed. Sam would answer a serious question in kind, though to see the expression on his face and the twinkle in his eyes made it obvious that he loved to mess with people.

It's amazing how few people never really pay any attention to those they speak with. They only hear a response, awaiting an opening so they can speak. Sam seemed to enjoy people and tried to evoke something fun with his responses. I could only hope I was a worthy adversary, or possibly an accomplice.

"Sam, you can't mess with eagles unless you are Native American. I thought you were Italian. I guess you must belong to the Awopahoe tribe. I have never eaten eagle, but heron is delicious. In fact, it's a tradition in my family that every New Year's Eve we eat pickled heron. I am of German descent, and I think it might be a custom that was brought over from the Old Country that we continue. It's supposed to bring you good fortune throughout the coming year."

It was Sam's turn to laugh. "I think you mean herring, pickled herring."

"Whatever, Sam, you eat your eagle and let me and my family eat our heron."

We both laughed.

I poured us both another cup. "I hope you don't mind your coffee black 'cause I ain't got no cream, and I ain't got no sugar, though I might be able to find some booze if you'd like."

Sam told me that black was fine, a good thing because I didn't have any booze either. "Dan, I know you're writing. Did I ever tell you about the article I had published?"

I pretended that it was the first time I'd heard this proclamation of his so-called published story.

"No. You really had something published? What was it about?"

Sam said he had the magazine with the article in it someplace in his camper and that he'd find it and bring it over for me to read sometime.

"Sam, I would love that."

He continued, "It was about dogs, in particular a couple of dogs I owned that I used to hunt with. It was in a magazine dedicated to dogs and bird hunting. I used to love bird hunting and watching those dogs even more so than shooting. Once a dog gets onto the scent of its quarry, it really is an amazing thing to watch. They start out with their nose in the air till they find that scent then put it to the ground and follow it, moving back and forth till they come close, and their progress slows the closer they get."

Sam was smiling and it was obvious by the way he talked and the way he was acting that he was reliving the feeling and the times he spent with his dogs, watching them as they got ever closer to their quarry and he anticipating his dogs finding it.

"Dan, it was beautiful just watching them, and often I would let them flush those birds, really not even caring about shooting them, but when I didn't, my dogs looked at me almost as if disgusted with *my* failure. They did what they were supposed to, and I didn't hold up my end. Do you hunt at all, Dan?"

"I have shot a few pheasants though not often. Now I don't hunt anything anymore. I used to hunt deer. That is until I bought my house. Now the deer come into my yard and they're more like pets than wild animals. I now find myself enjoying their sight more than their taste. I guess I'm getting old and soft."

Sam asked if I had any dogs.

"No dogs, though I do have two cats. You told me you were too selfish to have kids. Well I suppose that's the same reason I don't have dogs. It would be too selfish of me. I work too much and I'm not home enough, and cats are just fine being home alone."

"You don't strike me as a cat person."

"What can I say? I love animals, though I probably would have agreed with you before I bought this house."

"And just what does buying a house have to do with you being a cat person?"

"I bought a foreclosed house and the previous owner had left behind two cats. So I suppose you could say those cats adopted me rather than the other way around. It was their house first after all."

"What are you trying to say, that it's their house and they let you stay?"

"I guess that's as good an analogy as any, and even better than that."

"You mean the best part isn't that you're a cat person? I cannot imagine how you could possibly top that."

"Sam, I think you are trying to insult me, but you are going to have to do a whole lot better than that to hurt my feelings. No, even better than the cats adopting me is that they pretty much named themselves."

"Now you're scaring me. Are you trying to tell me that your cats talk to you?"

"No, they don't talk to me, though by their actions, naming them was easy. One of my cats seems to have a problem with gas and it flatulates a lot."

"So what did you name it? Sir Fartsalot?"

"No, that would be downright silly, and let me assure you silly I'm not. I pride myself in having a certain air of class about me, a dignity that would not stoop to that level. If I let you think about it long enough, I know you'd come up with the same name. A cat that farts... a pussy passing air."

Sam sat there awaiting the name and commented that he already knew me well enough to know that my mind operated a little different from most people he had met.

"Queefer! Get it Sam? A pussy fart is a queef. Therefore, I named my cat Queefer! C'mon Sam, you gotta love it."

"I get it, Dan, and I can hardly wait to hear the other one's name."

I had the feeling that Sam was amused, but he acted as though he wasn't. I looked at him, kind of proud at my ability to "talk" to the animals, and I continued on with my explanation. "The other one is a female that always licks her nipples."

Sam gave me a look of one trying to seem interested. "Is this anything like the joke, 'Why does a dog lick his balls?'"

"No, Sam."

"The cat has been spayed and she doesn't produce milk, so I call her Milkdud or just Dudley for short."

Sam looked at me and shook his head. "Dan, you are a strange man."

"Why thank you, Sam. I'll take that as a compliment, and as I said they basically named themselves."

I asked him what his plans were for the day and he told me that today was an exercise day. Three times a week he'd go to the local gym with some other people from camp and today was one of those days.

"What is your goal, Sam, to someday enter a bodybuilding competition or to just stand in front of a mirror and admire yourself?"

Sam let out a rather loud "*Ha!*" "No, I try to push myself so I can keep what control I have for as long as possible and hopefully to keep myself going for a while longer. Exercise seems to help."

"Not only to have that, Sam, but you get to look at some nice hard buns of women who take pride in their bodies while on an exercise bike. How goes your battle with Huntington's?"

"Good. I seem to be maintaining. I am doing good. But I'm not too sure about the nice fannies on those bikes you are talking about. We are in South Florida after all, and most of the women who exercise down here are past the point of having a hard body. Exercise is more done so they can maintain what they have and not so much to get back the bodies of their youth."

I told Sam that one of the things I liked about this campground was how people seemed to be comfortable in their own skin. There were men with flabby bellies that didn't wear shirts and women in shorts with flabby thighs and broad behinds. Hard bodies were actually the exception. People in this place had become comfortable with both themselves and those around them. They didn't read fashion magazines and only were concerned with enjoying their life. It truly was a beautiful thing.

As we both sat there, Sam's leg would periodically just lash out. Even something that most of us take for granted, something as simple as sitting, Sam could not totally control. His body was in constant motion. His head would nod then snap right back. His arms sometimes would flail side to side. His legs crossed at the knees would sometimes result in the top leg just kicking out.

"Sam, the way that leg just lashes out on its own, I just gotta know, have you ever kicked someone in their nuts?"

Sam laughed. "I think you'll like this. I haven't kicked someone in the nuts but I have my own. Sometimes my leg kicks backwards as well. When I put on my pants I have to sit down, and yesterday morning my leg kicked back and caught me. I couldn't even stand up for a while after that."

We sat there drinking our coffee and even though Sam's body moved about, I was amazed that he didn't spill his coffee.

Someone I'd met the previous year pulled into my campsite. I say "pulled in." She was riding a bicycle.

Sam introduced her, "Dan, this is Jonie. She's from Michigan."

"Hi, Jonie from Michigan."

"Hi, Dan from New York. How have you been?"

"I am doing wonderful, and how have you been?"

Sam spoke up, "I take it you two have already met?"

I told him not to be jealous, that we had merely met the year before, that there was nothing between us, and I would not come between them. "That is unless you're looking for a threesome, Sam."

Jonie was probably in her seventies and maybe five foot tall, *maybe*, and on a good day, *if* she was wearing heels and standing on a platform. She always had a twinkle in her eye and her laughter, which was often, was that of a little school girl giggling. She was absolutely beautiful. She was considered a traitor by those in Rustic for moving to Electric and was told that if she ever rode her bike through this section again, she would be tied to the whipping post and flogged.

She rode in on her bicycle standing up. Honestly, I don't think she could have reached the pedals if she was sitting down. It was a woman's bike. If it had been a man's, I think maybe she would have been a little uncomfortable, or perhaps not. Having to straddle that crossbar might have made that twinkle in her eye even brighter and her giggle even louder. It might have been the ride of her life.

She looked over at Sam. "Don't forget dinner is at my place tonight around six."

"I remember, and thank you, Jonie. What should I bring?"

"Just you, Sam." She proceeded on her way.

I said to Sam that there seemed to be a lot of people here from Michigan. "Just what do you call yourselves? I am a New Yorker. Michiganders or Michigonians, perhaps Michiganites. Hey you are of Italian descent I guess you are a Michiginuien?"

"Dan, where I am from hardly dictates who I am."

We both smiled.

I said, "You seem to be a pretty popular guy around this place."

"There are a lot of good people here."

I added, "Good, yes, though apparently they are rather a poor judge of character insofar as they seem to like you."

We drank our coffee and he asked about my plans for the rest of the day.

"My only thoughts or plans for this time I am here are that I am going to fish, I am going to write, and I am going to enjoy this place and the people within it. Are you hungry? How 'bout some breakfast? I've got some bacon and eggs that need to be cooked and I'm kind of hungry."

"I'd like that. Thank you." He also said that if I didn't mind he'd like his bacon cooked "extra crispy." It was not bad for you if it was cooked all the way through, and it still tasted pretty good.

I toasted some bread over the flames and he asked me to not put any butter it. Sam sacrificed his taste buds, hoping to extend his life. His eggs I cooked "over easy."

Breakfast served. Breakfast eaten.

We parted our ways, Sam back into the campground and I out onto the high seas for a day of fishing. I headed into town for my day's supply of bait, wishing Terry a "top o' the morning to ya."

I stopped at a Deli and picked up some fried gizzards and beans with rice for lunch. Back at camp, I loaded up my gear into the boat and headed out onto the ocean.

I returned to land and cooked the fish caught, and afterwards I went into my camper and wrote...

[...]

At least I attempted to write.

I left both the campground and safety of land behind as I headed out into the ocean.

The seas, the tides were more than I was used to and in a small boat that was designed for small lakes...

No, dammit! It doesn't "feel" right.

...The sanctity of land left behind, I pushed the throttle of my boat fully forward and my boat skimmed over the waves as I left behind all of my problems and thoughts...

Aw, crap. This was not what I had anticipated.

This writing stuff wasn't as easy as I remembered it being. It seemed too forced. I was beginning to think that maybe writing was just another part of the life I perceived, the future I imagined.

What the hell. Tomorrow was another day, and so I went to bed.

Chapter 8

Star Light, Star Bright

It seemed as though I had no sooner gone to bed and had lain my head upon my pillow than I was already starting to awaken to the dawn of another day.

I do believe it was early in the A.M., maybe five o'clock. Or maybe it was only four, or possibly it was three? Perhaps it was already six, or maybe I had just fallen asleep and it was still in the P.M.

I guess I really had no idea of the time. I just felt that I had been asleep long enough.

What I did know was that the cobwebs of my slumber were still upon me even though I felt I had had enough sleep and was ready to welcome the start of a new day, or just perhaps my bladder was full and telling me I had to pee. Whatever the reason, I decided it was time for me to get my fanny out of bed.

I had prepared a pot of coffee the night before and stepped outside with that pot in hand. I turned on my outdoor stove and placed the pot upon the flames while I sat there anticipating the sounds of coffee perking. I suppose that I was still half asleep. My body may have been moving, although my mind wasn't quite there.

Outside there were no clouds in the heavens above and the stars stretched from one horizon to the other. With no lights from any city, nor smog from the traffic of those living there and the industry that kept people within those confines, the skies were not distorted from lights or pollution, and the magnitude of the heavens lay above and beyond me.

The stars were so dense that one star blended into the next, one constellation into another. They were so numerous that it made me realize what a little piss-ant I was, just another being or critter miniscule in the magnitude of the universe. I was left in awe of all the possibilities: life beyond me or this little piece of dirt we call Earth, just another rock that ran in circles around a star that we call the Sun. Our Sun is no different from any of the stars that we see. Why do so many people think our star is so much different from all of those, and our world the only one blessed by an unknown entity that someone wrote of long ago.

Sitting in the dark and being alone, I was able to see and wonder about the possibilities of what infinity could actually entail—the magnitude of the heavens, the universe never ending. What lay above me that I could see I knew was but a fraction of what lay beyond that, and if I could be at the edge of what I saw, I knew I could see the same beyond that.

Stars, and their prisms of light reflecting through our atmosphere, were the same as our own sun, and they too might have planets of their own. Being alone, with no distractions from my day-to-day life, I observed and enjoyed the possibilities of a Heaven, of a God, of life beyond mine and the rest of us who live on this rock running in circles around a heater that keeps us alive.

I looked at the constellations that I could identify. There was the Big Dipper that stood so prominent above me, and there was Orion's belt, a part of Orion the Hunter constellation, though I had no idea where the rest of him was, and I guess that was about all I could actually identify.

In my camper was a book my sister, Dee, had given me on stars and the constellations they formed. I even contemplated going to get it. Knowing their names would never enhance what I was looking at.

I adhere to no religion that someone else interprets from a book written by other men from long ago and that (I think) would be every religion. Every "good book" was written by a person. To follow that belief is to follow someone else's belief. There is no proof. That's why they call it faith.

Sitting alone with no distractions, all I knew was something existed beyond me and my life. I didn't need an intermediary to tell me how to commune with a God that I felt. I *know* there is something after this life, and that's good enough for me.

I try to be good, but it's not for any reward in the afterlife. I just like people, and I guess my reward is their friendship or maybe a mutual respect. We all know right from wrong, though too many people use religion to be "holier than thou," and they beat their chests and condemn those that don't follow their path. People die and kill in the name of their God, and if they really believed, they would know He needs no help from them.

Meteorites were common, shooting stars from the cosmos, and I never even contemplated a wish. They were but a pebble from the heavens falling to our earth, and just in seeing one my wish was being granted.

I lay there in my lounge chair for maybe twenty minutes, maybe two hours. Time was something that ceased to exist upon my arrival in the Keys; it was something I had left behind.

I came here to relax and not to contemplate the meaning of life. The pitter-patter of little feet brought me out of my thoughts. Okay maybe not little feet, and hardly a pitter-patter...

Sam had the feet of an adult even though his gait was almost that of a toddler first learning to walk. His pitter-patter days were since long gone. Sam's disease had lain its claim to so many aspects of his life, and his walking was probably the most obvious to those that did not know him.

To see him walk, many people thought he was a drunkard just staggering along. To talk to him was to know better. His speech, at least for the most part, showed the clarity of his mind. A child, when it first discovers walking, has more of a stagger or a somewhat controlled progress, or maybe not so much controlled as it is instinctive: one or two steps forward, a stagger to the side, sometimes a backward step, and again a step forward. The goal was what lay ahead.

It was the same with Sam, only he was aware of what his body should do, even though he was not always able to control more than just his forward progress, and he accepted that. Getting to his destination was enough, even if his destination was something as simple as arriving at my campsite for a cup of coffee and some conversation.

One or two steps forward, a step to the side, a pause, looking ahead. His head would drop down then snap back up. A stagger to the side and a step forward, a step back and a few more steps forward—the gait of a child and the determination of a man knowing his limitations, knowing he needed to push himself. To not do so would be to surrender and accept the road that had been paved before him by his ancestors with the disease he had inherited.

"Oh, Danny."

Hearing Sam's approach brought me out of my thoughts of the cosmos and the meaning of life. All right, maybe I was dozing off and Sam brought me back to the here and now.

"Good morning, Sam."

"Good morning, Danny."

I grabbed a mug that I had sitting on the picnic table and was about to pour Sam a cup of coffee when he interrupted me, "I brought my own cup, Dan," as he put it forth.

He claimed it was spill proof. I say spill proof, but with Sam it was only spill less. He still managed to allow some coffee to get away.

I was wearing a hooded sweatshirt with *U.S. Navy* emblazoned across the front that Sam looked at. "Dan, I didn't know you were a Navy man."

I replied, "No I am not. I am a fan of the Village People."

We drank our coffee and spoke of our pasts and more or less brought us both up to date on our lives till now. We shared a few memories.

I had a tree service company and busted my fanny for nine months of the year.

Sam, on the other hand, was retired and was doing the things he enjoyed. He camped and fished and enjoyed his life and all those he met along the way. He grew up in Grosse Point, a suburb of Detroit, Michigan, and had a Catholic upbringing. His education began in a school named St. Paul's. It was a Catholic elementary school, complete with nuns for teachers (or more appropriately, custodians of their wards).

I grew up in the town of Gates, a suburb of Rochester, New York, and went to St. Theodore's, a Catholic school as well.

Sam went on to an all-male high school that named St. Paul's Preparatory; I continued my education at Gates-Chili, a public high school. Upon his graduation from his "prepatory" high school, he went on to Michigan State University where he studied data processing and earned a degree in Marketing, temporarily staying out of the military that was claiming all the young men they could to send to Vietnam.

The government's war in Vietnam had ended, as well as the draft, before my graduation from my "formal" education, and I never had to make the decision on what I would do about the military and possibly dying for something I was too young to comprehend. (Now that I'm older I still don't understand.) I got married to my childhood sweetheart and we moved to Texas where I got a job working construction. The year was 1976.

For Sam it was still the time of the Vietnam war, and upon graduating from college, he joined the Navy to serve his country, hoping to avoid killing others and maybe dying for a cause he was unsure of. He was stationed in San Diego, teaching others what he had learned about data processing and computers.

I guess I wasn't capable of satisfying my wife's needs, or rather her desires, and she left me for another. She fell out of love. We were happily married for four years. One year of wedded bliss. One year of... whatever... and two years that I hadn't seen her until we signed our divorce papers. With no obligations, I decided to continue working construction.

Sam completed his obligation with the military and went to work for IBM, selling computers and their related software.

Me? What can I say? I again fell in love, again got engaged, and again got married, and being the ambitious person I was, I continued working construction.

Sam, on the other hand, left IBM and took a job with Coldwell Realty in their commercial department in San Diego.

I again headed to the divorce courts, my wife having rekindled a previous love, or at least someone she had screwed in the past. And me? I continued working construction.

Sam went from San Diego to Seattle with Coldwell, to an office they were opening for selling commercial real estate.

I again fell in love and again got engaged and (surprise, surprise), I continued working construction.

Sam established himself in Seattle as someone who could find both sellers and buyers of some pretty major properties.

Me? I didn't wait for my "love" to decide that it wasn't going to work. I was beginning to see that life wasn't just what I wanted it to be. I began to get over my naivete and called off the wedding... and I continued working construction.

Sam asked for details of my loves and my divorces.

"Sam, both me and my first wife were young. She didn't have much of a childhood. Her mother had terminal cancer when she was maybe ten or eleven, and she basically took over the household duties, or I guess they were forced upon her by a father that just didn't understand that she was so young. I suppose she just hadn't been given the chance to be a child and she had too many desires yet to explore. I think she was a good person. I forgave her the first time she strayed from our vows, and the second time I just bought her a one way ticket back to Rochester from Texas. Truth be told, I traded her for a hammer."

Sam looked at me, and I could tell by his expression that he had no idea just what in the hell I was talking about. "You traded your wife for a hammer?"

"Yes. Though if I might add, and to my credit, it was a really good hammer!"

I went on to explain that my wife had left for someone I considered my "brother." He was a very close friend and he had left his hammer in my garage after helping me with a project.

"They did not stay together very long. I still have that hammer that he had left in my garage. I do believe that I got the better end of the deal. It's a ball-peen hammer with a white fiberglass handle and a rubber grip, and like I said, Sam, it really is a good hammer. I still have that hammer and he doesn't have her. It was a good trade.

"My second wife I thought was my soul mate, though it was a sad day when I realized she had no soul. She used to be so proud of the fact that she could count on one hand just how many men she had slept with, and I suppose she still can, but I have to believe that one hand was holding a calculator. How about yourself?"

Sam and his wife never had a single argument other than him wanting her to go to work. "It's the only thing we ever argued about. I wanted her to get a job. She liked the good life; she liked being pampered."

Sam said that a friend set him up on a blind date that he didn't even want, but after a bit of persuasion, he agreed. "I was perfectly content in my dating life and the women I was seeing. I cared about them and they cared about me, but there was never any commitment, and it was accepted and appreciated in the honesty on both our parts. I was never in love and it was nothing I ever even imagined. I really had no concept of the meaning of it until I laid my eyes on her—Dan, it was love at first sight. Between her smile and personality, the way she interacted with others, I was done with the dating scene. This was the only woman I wanted to be with."

We sat there for a little while and it was obvious that Sam was reflecting on a love now gone. The smirk, or rather the half smile, I knew was a reflection of his memories.

"They only time we ever argued was about me wanting her to get a job."

I asked him if he wanted her to work was because he realized he had this disease and there would come a time when he could no longer work.

He never answered; he never acknowledged my question. And I never asked again.

We went on to talk of our upbringing and our Catholic education, something we had both somehow managed to survive.

"Sam, those nuns were pretty amazing. A perceived infraction brought out that ruler. I swear they must have had training from a martial arts instructor. They were as proficient as any

Samurai warrior with his sword. That ruler would appear out of nowhere, having been hidden within the folds of their robes and ready to strike at a moment's notice. It was an art I'm a tellin' ya, Sam!"

Sam let out his "Ha!" and told of his experiences. "I remember one time this nun caught me chewing gum. She grabbed me by the collar of my shirt and snatched me right out of my chair. It was amazing how such a small woman could possess such power, such strength. The speed with which she moved I still am in awe of. She made me take that gum out of my mouth and stick it on my nose, and it stayed there all day. She had that ruler in hand and told me to bend over and said those words that we've all heard before: 'You know, this is going to hurt me much more than it's going to hurt you.'

"I was bent over a chair and made the mistake of looking at her and saying, 'No it isn't.' The look on her face changed from one of anger to one of what I can only describe as joy, and she said so matter of fact, 'You know what, Samuel? You are correct. I think you will feel this much more so than I, and she proceeded to crack that ruler across my ass harder than ever before."

"Before that, I never remember her smiling, and every time thereafter, whenever she looked at me, she had a smile and a look in her eye that would just dare me to say something."

I had to laugh in the knowing just what those nuns were capable of and I asked, "And what grade was that in, Sam?"

"I think it was my second year of college."

I looked at him, the expression on my face I'm sure showing my surprise as he burst out laughing, knowing that I had believed him.

"No, it was probably the fourth or fifth grade. The college spankings were usually with a bare hand, and they weren't done by any women dressed as penguins. Well, okay maybe only one time, though in my defense I was young, and it was in my college years."

It was my turn to let out a laugh. I told him that a few of the people that worked around here probably would have made good nuns. "Christa up front has a very professional demeanor, kind of a no-nonsense attitude that makes sure people know it's all business, even though beneath that facade lies a heart of gold. I think that she would have made a good nun. In fact, I think I'll start calling her Sister Christina Marie from now on."

Sam piped in, saying that Brenda would make a wonderful Mother Superior, and I said that the owner of the establishment, Joann, could be the nun who had retired and sat in the nunnery praying to her Lord and that someday she would probably be appointed to Sainthood.

Sam said that a miracle had to be attributed to her first.

"Sam, just the fact that she likes you, I would have to consider that alone an act of divine intervention."

"Dan, I owe you a breakfast. Let's go to out to eat."

I said, "I've still got bacon and eggs, and it's a whole lot cheaper than any restaurant."

I got out the bacon and cooked it extra crispy. The eggs I poached in some boiling water while I toasted some bread on the grill—no butter for Sam on his toast, I remembered.

He tried to maintain every aspect of his health to live a functional life as long as he could. All right maybe not every aspect. He did partake of a few cocktails periodically.

Was I currently dating anyone, he asked? I told him that, other than an occasional date from the Internet, no. I mentioned a previous customer who had seen me on a date site and had contacted me. "We decided to go out one night and we had a really wonderful time, dinner followed by a few cocktails, and I spent the night at her house. The following day I called her to say what a wonderful time I'd had, and all she said was, 'I don't want to talk about it.' When I told her that I really enjoyed her company, the only thing she said was, 'I drank too much.'"

Sam let out a "Thank God for alcohol," and I let out a "Glory Hallelujah!" He followed with, "Can I have an Amen!" and I proclaimed, "Amen, my brother."

We both laughed and he asked if I was going to fish that day. I told him that indeed I was. "Come on by tonight and I'll have some fish for supper."

Sam looked at me. "You seem a little cocky in saying you'll be successful in bringing some fish back."

"It's an ocean full of fish to be caught, not necessarily those that inspired big bucks in the restaurants, but something for table fare at the very least. With a little patience and the right bait there is always something to be caught."

He declined, saying that he already had been invited to dinner at someone else's place.

We parted ways, he back to his camper, probably for a nap, and I into town for some bait and out onto the seas for a day of fishing.

I returned to shore with enough fish for the evening's dinner. Fish on the grill with some rice and beans, a few beers, and a little conversing with my neighbors, and I was done.

I had a full belly and an empty mind, and that was a most terrible thing to waste. I headed into my camper with my notes, trying to write, and fell asleep to visions of sugarplums dancing in my head.

Chapter 9

A "Nun" Too Good a Guide

I awoke the next morning and looked about my camper to more than a few empty beer cans, as well as wadded-up scraps of paper, strewn about upon the floor.

I had tried to continue with my book from the previous year, but the words I put on paper did not seem worthy of the story I was trying to write. My night had been restless, my mind being filled with not only the thoughts of that book but trying to put those thoughts into written words. The ink would find paper, and the paper would find the floor. I had a story in my mind that had seemed so clear before, but seemed to no longer be there.

The previous year, creativity had found me through writing, and I thought upon my arrival in the Keys it would return. Creativity is a strange creature. It was so simple the year before. A thought would turn into written words with little or no effort, as if I was merely a conduit of thoughts that in turn would find their way onto paper, as if something totally beyond me was doing the writing.

Maybe it had come too easily. Writing was suddenly difficult; it was too forced. It wasn't what I remembered. Oh, but the life of a wannabe writer: restless nights and empty beer cans and the destruction of trees that have been turned into paper only to find its way into the dumpster.

Those that adhere to being "green" would not like me. I seem to go through a lot of trees.

I guess it was like being a child again, wondering if Santa would bring me what I had been hoping for, or would it be like the time I had discovered Santa's hiding place, only to ruin Christmas morning and the unwrapping of my gifts?

When we stop having a goal or a dream, when we no longer look to the future, we accept our lot in life, and I think our death begins, or at least we stop living. My book was my goal, and as long as I continued to write, it kept my dream alive, the dream of something beyond my own existence, a future of something better. Maybe a story that would live long after me.

Sitting outside as the stars began to fade, I was at a point in my life where I still had dreams, though they were not quite the same as those in my youth. A writing of some story that was in my head was about it, and it was enough to keep me excited with the potential of its completion.

The sounds of Sam's footsteps coming around the bend made me realize that what I had was pretty damn good. I was okay with my lot in life. My life really isn't so bad, new friends and the old stories they shared that were new to me, their memories possibly becoming stories I would share with others.

Sam sat down at my picnic table and I got off my lounge chair and sat across from him, pouring him a cup of coffee.

"Sammy, good morning."

"Hi, Danny."

Sam enjoyed reading *USA Today*. He claimed that it seemed pretty much as unbiased in its political views or stories as any decent paper out there, and he had brought a copy of that day's paper along with him. He set it down on the table and took a sip of his coffee.

"Sam, how long have you been awake that you've already got today's paper?"

He went on to explain that he was normally awake by 5:00 A.M. Although his medicine made him sleep a lot, he still was awake early every morning.

He already had a section of paper in hand and I picked up one as well. We sat there drinking our coffee and reading.

He wanted to know about my hobbies and told me that he loved skiing and asked if I ever went.

"I have gone a few times, though I guess I wouldn't be considered an avid skier."

"Was that downhill or cross-country?"

"Cross-country. I really enjoy the solitude of being in the woods amongst nature. Though I've gone downhill and I did like the thrill of it, I think I enjoy cross-country more."

"I tried cross-country a few times, but I didn't really like it," he said. "The excitement of downhill I found absolutely amazing, the thrill of always being on the edge of my limits made me feel alive. I used to go probably thirty times a year. I even went so far as to try helicopter skiing a couple of times. A friend of mine had gone before, and listening to his stories of the thrill and beauty of skiing on virgin snow that you had to be brought to by a helicopter, I knew it was something that I had to do.

"I immediately booked a trip at this place that he'd gone to at a resort up in Canada. It was even better than he had described. It was everything and anything that I could have possibly imagined. They would load us into a helicopter and bring us up to an elevation of maybe ten thousand feet and drop us off with a guide. I really wasn't that good of a skier. In fact, I was probably way out of my league.

"We were in areas prone to avalanches, and our guide would explain the route we'd be taking and that we were to follow him. He stressed that to not do so could very well lead to our deaths. It was virgin snow, no tracks or trails to follow. The snow had never been skied on before. It was wonderful."

It was fun to see Sam and his expressions as well as to listen to him. In his telling of the adventure it was as if he was reliving it and I was along for the ride.

"Sam, you plead a good case for downhill. It does sound like it could be a whole lot of fun, though I can't even relate. I think I'll stick to the woods and cross-country."

He continued. There was one time he didn't follow the guide's lead and ventured out on his own. He had been caught up in enjoying both himself and the thrill of skiing on the very edge of his limits. "I guess I was enjoying the thrill and not paying any attention. Dan, when we got to the bottom of the hill that guide was really pissed at me. He said that I was lucky to even be alive. He told me that I could have caused an avalanche that could have killed not only me, but all of us. I was chastised; I was berated. I felt almost as if I was back in school being scolded by the nuns. The only thing missing was the yardstick across my ass."

Sam talked of the thrill of always being on the very edge of wiping out and how much fun it was. He also said that several times he was skiing way above and beyond his level of expertise.

Well, to that I said "bullshit!" Sam *was* skiing at that level. Helicopter skiing is considered an extreme sport, one which requires both physical and mental skills most cannot comprehend, let alone attempt. I guess a set of brass balls doesn't hurt either, and I'm sure that Sam had himself a set.

He said he'd gone three different times, each of those times for one week. Every morning a helicopter would pick them up, bring them to the top of a mountain, and drop them off to ski to the bottom. Oftentimes it would be repeated, depending on the time it took them to complete their journey, a helicopter picking them up at the bottom of a mountain they had skied down, only to bring them to the top of another.

Sam sat there for a few moments and then said, "Dan, let me buy you breakfast today."

"I'll tell you what. We'll go tomorrow, and I might even let you buy. For today, I've still got some eggs in the fridge and some refried beans left from last night."

Sam grumbled that he owed me, and I told him that if I didn't cook it today, I'd have to throw it away tomorrow.

I threw some scrambled eggs, refried beans, and cheese on a tortilla and Sam quit his bellyaching and proclaimed how wonderful my cooking was. I enjoyed cooking, and Sam enjoyed eating. We both loved talking. It was exactly what a vacation is supposed to be: newfound friends sharing old stories and creating new ones.

Me and Sam parted our ways, he into the campground and I headed to the showers and then into town for some bait for fishing. I got in my boat and was back out onto the ocean for some fun in the sun.

When running a business, your life for the most part revolves around others and their needs. When away from that, it leaves the world open to your own thoughts and your own needs. I didn't have any needs, or rather they were few so I was left to my own thoughts and my own desires, for better or worse. It was wonderful.

A few fish were cleaned and put in the freezer up at the store to take to my people back home. I cooked supper. I decided on a steak for the grill, with some potatoes sliced and cooked in olive oil. A few people and a few conversations, as well as a few beers, later I retired to my camper with my pen and paper and my notes.

I went to sleep smiling, with my notes lying next to me.

Chapter 10

Consuelo's Cantina

I knew of Sam's impending arrival well before he announced his presence. The coral that ground beneath his feet could be heard even before he could be seen roundin' the bend.

I was sitting at my table when he showed up and I stood with my pot of coffee in hand as Sam sat down, and even before I could pour him a cup he told me in no uncertain terms that today he would be buying breakfast.

I said my piece. "Sit down, Sam. Coffee is cheap and your company is absolutely, positively priceless. You don't owe me nuthin', and I will be cooking breakfast."

I could tell that Sam didn't like my response and said to him that if my cooking was all that bad that I'd not do it for him again and we'd try one of his local restaurants.

"Dan, your cooking is GREAT."

"Sam, you have hurt me deeply, and you can kiss my entire ass." And with my next breath I said, "So where are we going to eat?"

There was a place up the road called The Galley that Sam had frequented in the past. A few cups of coffee and a few stories shared and I headed to the showers to make myself presentable for my date.

I got my truck and picked up Sam as we headed into town so he could pay what he considered his debt. I say we headed into town, but in actuality the Keys are a series of islands connected by one road, and the campsite lacked no necessities in their store for those camping there (plus a whole lot more), so there really was no need to leave other than for a change of scenery.

Many of the "towns" had a store or two, maybe a restaurant or a gas station, and maybe even a bait shop. Many of the islands were just a means to connect the bridges leading to the next and some only had mangrove trees on them.

Most of rural America is connected by roads. The Keys are not much different from that, though the roads have a few bridges connecting those towns, and those towns are different islands, or rather Keys, and it's only a bridge that separates them—a bridge and a span of water.

The town was a small part of most of the islands that lay along U.S. 1. The restaurant Sam chose was a few bridges and a few Keys away. We went on to the next island and the next and continued on until we arrived at the place where he wanted to go.

It was like a lot of places in the Keys that served good food and looked—for all intents and purposes to anyone not familiar with the lifestyle of the Keys—not too fancy. Most tourists would consider it quaint.

The Florida Keys are made up of a whole lot of people living their dream, as well as the tourists who support that dream, and the facades of buildings often reflect the prices. Those who only look at the outside are the same ones who judge people by their looks. Restaurants rise and fall as often as the dreams of those that open them, and to judge the quality of the food they serve by the outside of that place is as sad as judging a person without knowing them. A fancy front always means a fancy price. A crappy front might be a reasonable price, even though the food served could be excellent at either one, or equally bad.

We pulled into the parking lot.

"Dan, there's hardly ever room to park in this place. Usually you can't even get close."

We parked and headed into the restaurant, or rather tried to. Of course there were parking places available. The place was closed!

I looked at Sam and smiled. "What do you think? If it's that hard to get a parking spot, maybe we should just wait here till they open tomorrow."

He told me that they were closed one day a week and apparently this was that day. I told him that I needed to buy some coffee for back at camp. He said that he knew of a place further up the road that sold some wonderful coffee beans, so we continued up the road looking for a place that was open.

Up ahead and on our right I noticed a restaurant with a parked police car out front and said to him, "What do you think? If it's good enough for the local cops, they must have good food."

Sam's response, "Either that or they have really good donuts!"

That was good enough for me, and we pulled into the parking lot. The name of the place was Consuelo's Cantina.

Sam and I were seated by the hostess, and after sitting I asked Sam, "Do you know what they call a Spanish woman with no legs?"

He looked at me and shook his head, "No, Dan. Though I'm afraid to ask, I will. What is it that they call a Spanish woman with no legs?"

I looked at him and laughed. "Consuelo." I emphasized the syllables. "Get it? You have to say the name slowly."

"I get it, Dan."

I was proud of myself. Sam shook his head. "Dan, you are a strange man."

I took that as a compliment. "Why, I thank you, Sam."

It was a Cuban restaurant and their special was *huevos rancheros*, and like they say, when in Rome...

We both ordered their special and Sam had a coffee, black. I had the Cuban coffee or rather *café con leche*. As I said, when in Rome...

Our food was brought to us and we sat there eating and talking. Sam and I both liked talking. He let his mouth and food get in the way of his breathing. It was another part of his disease taking control. Breathing while eating while talking did not always go according to plan for Sam.

Sam's food went down the wrong way and he began to gag. I found it a nice break from his incessant talking and I, for a brief moment, enjoyed the respite.

Sam couldn't breathe and after watching him gasp for a few seconds, I decided to move in. This would probably be my only opportunity to physically abuse him with no recourse. I got behind him wrapping both arms around him and took my fist, thrusting it into his solar plexus just under where the ribs came together. He immediately coughed up his food.

I followed that by a good ole open-handed hard crack on his back for good measure and to make sure everything was dislodged. Sam's face was red and he sat there trying to catch his breath and breathe normally.

"Sam, I am glad you're paying. I think I would have been pissed seeing you not enjoying the food if it was on my tab."

"Thanks, Dan."

"Any time at all, Sam. Let me assure you it was my pleasure."

I gave him the biggest smile I could.

Sam liked talking as much as I. I had to be careful when I asked him something or said something that he would respond to, because he would always respond.

I told him about the time I'd been to Guatemala and stayed with a friend of mine, Pablo, and his family. Their language was Spanish. "The beer we would drink there was called *El Gallo*, which translated means a male rooster. That meant that we were drinking a cock."

He didn't think I was right either.

We continued with our meal, with me trying to not talk too much because it resulted in Sam responding, whether or not he was eating. I noticed a sign on the wall in back of us that read, *Help wanted. Waitress needed.*

"Hey, Sam, they are looking for a waitress here. Why don't you move on down here and live year round? You would make a good waitress."

Sam looked at me and said that if he did, he would put on a skirt and change his name to Consuelo and he would even shave his legs.

Our meal finished, our waitress asked if we'd like dessert. She described the various pastries that were on display in a case right next to Sam, one of them being flan.

He declined, saying he was too full, though both the description and sight of the food just over his shoulder was weighing heavily on his mind.

I made it even worse. "Just look at that flan. How can you resist it?" Our waitress assured us it was homemade. In fact, it was a house specialty and she had made it herself that very morning. "Sam, take a look at that. You can almost taste it with your eyes."

I could tell he was debating, and he finally said, "I'm just too full, Dan."

I motioned for the waitress to give me the bill.

"Sorry, señor, it's already been taken care of."

I looked at Sam and he just smiled. "I told you I was buying."

"Okay, you got me this time, but the next one is on me."

We went outside. Sam stopped before we got to my truck and looked back at the restaurant, seeming a little anxious. He was moving about a little more than usual, shifting his weight from one foot to the other, and it reminded me of a child having to pee.

I asked, "Sam, what's the matter, do you have to use the restroom?"

He hesitated for a second before responding. "No, I'm thinking about that flan."

I burst out laughing. He explained that another part of his disease was that once a thought came into his mind, sometimes he couldn't let it go, and the thought of that dessert was almost too much for him.

I said to him that because he had given me that little tidbit of information, I might just have to use it against him in the future. I also told him that maybe by the time we got to the coffee shop, his appetite might be ready to accommodate his desires and he agreed.

"Sam, they must have more than just gourmet coffee. I am sure they also have tasty treats."

The coffee shop's name was Baby's, and it was just a few islands away from Key West. I chose their beans marked "breakfast blend." I brought it to the counter to have it ground, where they asked me how I made my coffee.

"Perked."

She wanted to know even more. "Is your coffee pot electric or on the stove?"

"Stove top."

Sam found a dessert of Key lime pie on a stick and we both left happy.

I was amazed that the difference in the way coffee is ground could make such a difference in the taste. It was a wonderful discovery to someone who enjoys the taste without any of the crap so many people put into it.

I often wonder why people don't just drink some sugar with caffeine and add a little something else. Oh yeah, I forgot. The younger generation has got it figured out. It's called an energy drink.

It was another glorious day in the Keys, and driving along U.S. 1 looking over the ocean with a newfound friend was about as good as it gets in my world.

We returned to camp and I thanked him for breakfast and told him that I owed him one. It was to be a point of contention, though it was a good one.

Sam was sitting at his picnic table, and after leaving the restrooms, I sat down across from him.

There was no wind, no breeze and the "No See Ums" were on a feeding frenzy. With the right background you could actually "See um." Within the confines of the campground there were times when those little bastards just seemed to be all over you, biting away. Even with it being eighty-plus degrees, I had on a long-sleeved shirt.

Sam sat there swatting at the bugs that feasted on his flesh. "Dan, aren't you hot in that shirt?"

No See Ums can find the smallest of openings to attack, and my shirt just left less exposed skin. Sam was beating himself up trying to ward the bugs off.

"Sam, my shirt helps to keep both the sun off me and gives the bugs a little less to gnaw on."

Sam almost screamed out, "Take your shirt off, YOU PUSSY!"

I burst out laughing as I told him, "You are what you eat," and I called him a cock while I laughed my ass off, with Sam beating himself up while swatting at bugs that couldn't be seen and me pretending to not be bothered at all, although they seemed to love the taste of my flesh as much, if not more so, than his. I left saying, "I'll talk to you later."

The only response that he could make to me was "okay, buddy" while he continued to swing and swat away at bugs that were gone by the time you felt their bite.

I asked if he had any plans for dinner that evening and, lo and behold, he had none. "I just happen to have an opening this evening as well, and if you'd like, dinner will be served at six or so."

He wanted to know at what time "six or so" meant.

I said, "Between 6:00 and 6:30. Why don't we call it 6:23?"

After that, I tried to organize my notes into some reasonable facsimile of the book that dwelled in my mind. It just wasn't happening. Several people stopped by and I took a tour of the campground, visiting with others. I even managed to squeeze a nap in. Damn, but this vacationing stuff really was rough.

That evening Sam stopped by with beer in hand. A six pack, actually.

"What is that, Sam? You usually bring a bottle of wine to your other dinners."

"That I do, but I didn't think you were the wine type of person."

He had read me correctly. I was more of a beer man. I told him that when I was a little bit younger, I drank Jack Daniels and had a boss that had discovered Cognac. "Sam, we'd get together and discuss the business and we'd have a few drinks. He poured me some of that stuff that cost forty dollars a bottle and when I didn't like it, he said, 'Dan, it's an acquired taste. Give it a chance.'

"I asked him, 'Just why in the hell would I want to learn to like something that cost forty dollars when I like something that cost ten?' He had no answer and knew I was right, and I think his Cognac probably was not quite as tasty after that. And that, Sam, is why I am more of a beer person."

He wanted to know what was for dinner, and I told him that it'd be fish cooked on the grill over charcoal. I asked how he'd like it cooked.

"Any way but well-done."

I'd always cooked fish well-done and Sam said that he didn't really like it that way. After cooking it the way he wanted, I had to agree.

After a few beers and some conversation, we both went our separate ways, Sam back to his camper and me into mine with a pen and paper. I managed to write a few pages for my book. Those too would eventually find their way into the dumpster.

Chapter 11

Toe-mas

Another morning arrived along with the dawn of a new day and possibly a new beginning. With it also came along the same ole Sam.

By that I mean he was the same Sam to those who knew him, but he was someone new to me. I was new to him as well, and we both had our own same old stories to share that were new to each other.

It was a wonderful way to start a day. I was sitting outside with the coffee pot on the table and a cup in my hand doing nothing in particular.

"And a top o' the morning to ya, Sammy me boy."

"Hi, Danny."

And so our day began.

Sam told me how much he had enjoyed the previous night's meal and how wonderful a cook I was. I told him that I knew he just loved eating and having his very own personal chef, and that he was only blowing smoke up my ass so that I might cook for him again.

I really do enjoy cooking, Sam truly does love eating, and we both thought we were getting more out of the deal than the other. We enjoyed each other's stories and our conversations. I felt a kindred spirit with him, something I had no experienced in a very long time.

We sat there drinking our coffee and a fell camper that I had not previously met stopped l

Sam introduced us. "Dan, this is Tom."

I stuck out my hand, anticipating a handshake. Tom just held my hand as he looked into my eyes and only said, "Hi, Dan, I am Toe-*mas*." (his pronunciation)

The name Thomas had been changed to protect the innocent I guess. He held my hand until I pulled it away.

We made small talk about where we were both from and different things for a little while, and gradually our conversation found its way into the teachings and philosophies of Aristotle and Socrates, or maybe it was our thoughts on the possibilities of life being found beyond our own planet. More than likely, it was just about the weather. I don't remember, and Tommy boy continued on his way.

Sam looked at me. "So, Dan, what are your feelings about Tom?"

"Well, Sam, he does seem like a nice enough fellow."

Sam just looked at me knowing that I was holding something back. "And?"

"And what, Sam?"

"And, Dan... I think you aren't saying what you really think."

I looked at him, trying to feign my innocence. "Like I told you, he seems like a nice enough person, a rather pleasant fellow, if I may add. Why would you wonder if there's anything else?"

Sam said he knew me well enough by now to know there was something I wasn't sharing.

He was right. "And he's gay, Sam, though hiding it, and he's not hiding it very well."

Sam looked at me, obviously not happy with my response. "Why the hell would you make that assumption!"

"Do not get me wrong, Sam. I could not care any less if Tommy boy is gay or straight. It really has no effect on me at all. He could be black or white, red, brown, yellow, or even pink. His religion might be a Catholic, Protestant, Muslim, or Jew. A Democrat or Republican, or whatever the hell he chooses, as long as he's good people and doesn't push his agenda on me or someone that doesn't want to hear it. Toe-mas being a turd burglar really doesn't matter to me. In fact, Mr. Sam, a gay guy is one less guy in competition with me, and *if* he is in fact successful, then that would be two less guys out there vying for the attention of some of God's most beautiful creations—women."

Sam shook his head. "Dan, I think you are being a little presumptuous, and if I may add, you are being a little bit too judgmental."

"Well, first off he goes by his formal name, not Tom, not Tommy, not even Thomas. He calls himself Toe-*mas*, for cryin' out loud! Who the hell goes by their formal birth name other than someone who's gay?" I paused and let Sam think for a moment. "Tell me that, Samuel."

I emphasized his formal name of Samuel, and he sat there for a moment before I continued with my rant.

"Samuel, there is something about his whole demeanor that screams out, I LIKE MEN, BROADWAY PLAYS, MADONNA, AND LADY GAGA!—the way he looks, the way he acts, the way he stares into your eyes as he's talking to you. I had the impression that he wanted to devour me."

"Dan, let me assure you that you are not that desirable to either of the sexes," Sam said.

I continued, "He wears those goofy shorts all the time that bicyclists wear. They are so tight that their crotches bulge out almost as if they are trolling for attention to their genitalia. *And*, not only that, he doesn't even ride a bicycle! Those shorts alone proclaim, *Hey girl!*"

"I guess you are right about those shorts. They are awfully tight, and bicyclists must always be cold." Sam kept trying to defend Toe. "Hey, what about Hungarian Jack? He wears nothing but Speedos, not even a shirt, and I'm pretty sure that he likes women, at least he seems to be in love with his wife."

"He's European, Sam. That doesn't count. Europeans aren't hung up on nudity or sexuality. They tend to live and let live. I think they are a little more evolved than us. Did you even notice the way Tommy's eyebrows went up when you farted? He smiled and moved even closer to you. Sam, he was thinking of your fanny and your bunghole."

Sam acted as if he wasn't amused. "Dan, two years ago he was down here with his wife."

"Really, Sam, do you really believe that? That's nice, and because he said it was his wife that made it true? Unless you attended the wedding, I have my doubts. Maybe you were his best man? Like I said, Sam, I could be wrong, though it would probably be only the third time in my life."

Sam laughed. "You know, Dan, I think you're right. I've always thought he was a fudge packer."

I burst out laughing. Sam found the good in people and would point out only those traits, though I think we'd gotten to a point where he trusted me not to repeat some of his thoughts and the conversations we shared.

He invited me back to his place for breakfast, and knowing he no longer cooked, I of course accepted, wondering what the hell I was in for. He headed back to his place and I told him to I'd be there in a little bit.

Arriving at Sam's, I sat down at his table, awaiting my meal, and Sam put forth a bowl of... of... something.

"Sam, this is... interesting. Just what the hell is it?"

"Yogurt and granola, Dan. It's good for both the mind and body."

I looked at it and shook my head. "Sam, if your mind and body is any indication of its rewards, I'm a thinkin' it ain't a workin'."

Sam was in good shape both mentally and physically, though I was not about to tell him that. "Hey, how about some poached eggs on toast to go along with your wonderful gourmet meal. I think that it might actually enhance it."

Sam said, "Or, we could go out for breakfast."

"Bite me, Sam. Let's finish this... this... stuff, this stuff that's good for our mind and soul, and maybe eat something that's good on the palate and a little more filling."

"Thanks, Dan, but this is good enough."

I already knew that once he got a thought in his mind, it kind of latched on to his very being, a combination of his disease taking over and his analytical mind. He was one of those people who saw a problem and dissected it every which way until he came up with the best possible solution. It was the reason he was successful in both business and in life. I think it was also the reason that he had kept his disease at bay for as long as he had. He did what was necessary to maintain his life.

Sam was easy to persuade to do what he really wanted to, and even though he was being polite in the declining of my offer, it was a losing effort.

"Sam, poached eggs on rye toast will complement your health food. Poached eggs are so wonderful when they are properly cooked." I realized that I was messing with him, teasing him with something he enjoyed.

Once I put that thought in Sam's mind he couldn't stop thinking of it. The more comfortable I became with Sam, the more I found to mess with.

"C'mon, Sam, let's go eat."

We headed over to my site. I grabbed an iron skillet, put a little bit of olive oil in it, sliced up some onions and a few potatoes, let them cook till they were done, and added a little corned beef hash into the mix. A few poached eggs and some bread charred over the flames and breakfast was served.

We sat there eating and Steve stopped by. He was from Ontario, Canada, where he was a fishing guide (he owned a charter service). He came down every winter with his wife, Wendy. Steve had a love and knowledge of fishing that I am sure transitioned into a successful business. I suppose he came here in the winter because he needed a break from his fellow Canadians and their being so nice all the time. What better way to want to get back to Canada than the abuse given to him by his neighbors, the Pirates, that he camped across from. The Pirates were a bunch of old bikers from Wisconsin that had probably been friends since they had gotten their first pubies.

"Hey, how would you guys like some fish. I caught some Yellow Jack yesterday that I just cleaned."

I'd never heard of Yellow Jack, and Steve explained that it was wonderful if cooked fresh.

"Well, hell yes, I'd love it."

Steve gave us the fish. Sam and I thanked him and he went on about his merry way.

"Sam, if it's fresh, it's good. What are you doing for dinner tonight? If you'd like, I'm a thinking that tonight I might cook up some tofu and bean curds to go along with your yogurt and granola diet along with that fresh fish Steve gave to us."

Sam told me he had a prior reservation with fellow campers. After a little while he went back to his camper to catch up on his beauty sleep, and I went into the campground to catch up on people.

I spent the day socializing with those I hadn't met and those I already knew, and before I knew it, the sun was on the horizon and my belly was letting me know it was in dire need of food.

I returned to my site hungry and invited my next door neighbors—my lesbian neighbors—over for dinner for some fresh Yellow Jack and they accepted. How could they not? Lesbians at the very least love the smell of fish. I know that's a dumb thing to say. It's right up there with the blind guy walking by the fish market saying, "Hello, ladies."

Their names were Latona and Linda, and they really were wonderful people and great neighbors. We spoke well into the evening as they talked about how they had sold their home and were living in a customized van and traveling the country. They were pretty cool and enjoying a life and this beautiful country together.

It had been another wonderful day, and I didn't even attempt to write before I fell asleep.

Chapter 12

I Am Judas

The next morning I was awakened by the song of a "mocking bird," a rather annoying, raucous sound that this particular bird sang.

"Oh, DANNY, get your lazy ass up!"

This mocking bird had no problem in taking me up on my open invitation to come by and enjoy my coffee any morning.

Sam had a feel for people and he knew that my invitation was true, that I wasn't just saying it to be polite.

When I had told him to stop by for coffee, it was because I thought he was a good target for my humor—he actually seemed to enjoy it—and I was an easy target for him as well. It was a win-win situation. Sam got a morning's cup of coffee, and I got someone to share it with.

I was already awake, and he assumed I had also been for a while and was ready for some company.

"Good morning, Sam."

"Hey, buddy, good morning."

I poured him a cup of coffee and we sat there replacing the night's sleep by a new day, some caffeine, and conversation to get the day going.

I'm sure that he didn't need the coffee to get going, but I know that I did. Huntington's disease, or maybe Sam's medicine, left him sleeping a lot, though I do believe that it was his mind that made sure that he didn't waste too many moments when he was awake.

As we sat there enjoying our coffee, my neighbor Linda brought by a pile of homemade buckwheat pancakes. "Thanks for dinner last night, Dan."

I told her that I wasn't expecting anything in return for that meal, that she didn't have to do this, but she said that it was something they wanted to do.

"Dan, you would have gotten our pancakes even without your fish."

I introduced her to Sam and they both said their hellos. She left the plate and went back to her home.

I looked at Sam and asked him, "How was your dinner last night, Sam?"

He watched Linda leave and said, "Dan, it was a nice night with good people and the food was good as well. It really was a good night."

I had a feeling that he was wondering about that fish I had cooked for my newfound friends and neighbors. I told him that I ate that Yellow Jack for dinner last night and that Steve's judgment of that fish's taste had been correct. "Yellow Jack, when it's cooked fresh, is really wonderful. You should try it sometime, Sam."

Sam looked at me and the expression on his face let me know that he wasn't all that happy and that he thought I had done him wrong.

"Dan, Steve gave that fish to *us*! Don't tell me that you sold me out for a couple of women."

I smiled. "No, Sam, I didn't sell you out. I merely replaced you for the evening with a couple of lovely ladies. In fact, if you keep this up, I am thinking that they might love some coffee in the morning as well as a little conversation and might even appreciate me a little more than you seem to. I am beginning to believe you are only using me because you like my coffee, and I am really hurt.

"Not only that, Samuel, but you are not giving them the respect they deserve. They do have names after all. They are my neighbors, Latona and Linda. They are really nice people, and I do believe worthy of that fish, and you know what, Sam? Not only that, they thought I was a wonderful cook and appreciated me and my act of kindness. They are homeless after all, two people living in a vehicle looking for a place to park for a night or two."

I rubbed it in a little more. "Sam, I believe they're from the Northeast, Maine or possibly New Hampshire or one of those New England states, and I think that they are used to fresh seafood right off the docks from the fishing boat, and even better yet, Sam, they said they'd never had a more tasty fish. They really were in awe of the taste of Yellow Jack caught fresh and cooked on the grill. Sam, they actually said Yellow Jack cooked rare on the grill is not only good, it's GREAT. Call me Judas if you want, Sam. I sold my soul for thirty pieces of fish."

He continued to express his disappointment in my eating *our* fish without him and with two people that were total strangers. He stressed the fact that Steve had given *us* that Yellow Jack.

"Dan, I hardly think they are homeless. They have a fancy van that probably cost more than a lot of people's homes. I heard that they are traveling around the country living a dream. Just because they don't pay property taxes doesn't mean they're homeless."

I told him that Steve had told us that the fish had to be cooked fresh. If not, it would be a waste not only of Steve's generosity but an insult to those very fish that had been sacrificed for us to savor them caught that very day, not only the fish but to dear ole Mother Nature herself.

"Sam, give me a break. They really are nice people and they are my new neighbors, not only that, but when they asked how they could repay me, I told them that I only wanna watch, and they agreed."

"What do you mean by that, Dan, that you wanna watch?"

"They're lesbians, Sam, and I told them if they were serious about repayment, the only thing I ask in return is I really wanna watch."

"There you go again, Dan, assuming that someone is gay. Just because they are two women traveling around the country together and on their own, you assume that they are gay. Just because they have golf clubs and short hair and speak their mind, you assume they are gay. What is with you, Dan? Do you have gaydar?"

As so often Sam made me smile and I responded, "Only one of them has short hair, the other, long and wavy, and I don't even think they have any golf clubs. Actually, I wondered if they were gay, so instead of wondering, I asked them. In my world it's really no big deal whether they are or not. I just like people that are nice. Most people make assumptions, myself included. If I really want to know, or even care, I'll just ask. Two down-to-earth women traveling around the country together I thought that I'd ask them rather than wonder or assume. It really ain't a big deal what their sexual preference is.

"They told me that they were and when I told them that the only repayment I wanted was that I really wanna watch. I was referring to wanting to watch the two of them together. They took it literally and my 'wanna watch' was rewarded with an old beat up Timex watch that had probably been purchased at some garage sale and on its last legs. Sam, those two ladies are as much of a wiseass as you."

"Dan, for thirty pieces of fish, you sold your soul."

"Yes, Sam, and I was rewarded with some buckwheat pancakes, and I really think they are going to be absolutely, positively wonderful. Sam, fresh has an expiration date. I really was only doing the honorable thing."

He wondered if I really asked them if I could watch, and I told him, "No, Sam, I do have a little more class than that."

And he asked where I had been hiding it all this time. "Dan, you *are* a Judas. You betrayed me for a few fish."

"Sam, it was not a few pieces of fish. It was Yellow Jack. Dammit, Sam, it sure was good and I think that you really should try it sometime. If you want another cup of coffee, I suggest you try to be a little nicer to me. Not only that, but I happen to have some homemade buckwheat pancakes I might be willing to share."

Sam feigned his being pissed and we moved on. He had this morning's copy of *USA Today* with him.

We had our cups of coffee and both had a section of the newspaper in front of us as we sat there reading, Sam's head buried beneath his section to the point that I couldn't even see his head, and I suppose I was doing the same with my section.

I peered over the top of the paper. "Speaking of them there homos, I just happen to have an article in here stating how homosexuality has actually been discovered in the animal kingdom. It seems they can trace its origin as far back as to the dinosaurs. It seems to be, at least within the animal kingdom, accepted... I think."

Sam lowered his paper.

"I'm serious, Sam. It claims that some dinosaurs might have become extinct because were attracted to the same sex, and there are actually two known species that they've discovered that no longer bred. They have named the female species the Lickalotapus and a male species a Megasaurass."

Sam shook his head and raised his paper back up as he buried his head behind it.

"Hey, Sam, seriously I think you're going to love this story."

He again lowered his paper a little as his eyes peeked over the horizon of it. He said that it had better be good, that he was currently enthralled with an article pertaining to the current state of affairs in the country of Guatemala. "Or maybe it's about Guadalajara, or maybe it's about the Galapagos. Anyways, Dan, it has to be better than what I'm reading right now."

I went on to tell Sam about the article that was titled "Kentucky Fried Chicken sells fish, seeks Pope's blessing."

Sam put down his paper. The look on his face was of someone in awe of what I had just said. "Dan, you're KIDDING me." He almost screamed it out. "That's beautiful, what an incredible marketing strategy. Just think about it."

I had caught Sam's attention. "Well, Sam, it states that the president—yes, Sam, that would be *the* president—of KFC has sent a letter to the Vatican, to the Pope himself, Pope Benedict XVI, asking that his Holiness extend his personal seal of approval for this particular item on their menu as 'a way for your holy flock to keep a holy Lenten season.'"

Sam was more than a little excited about my discovery.

"Dan, that is absolutely wonderful, the marketing strategy. In fact it's already working. Today is Thursday, yesterday was Ash Wednesday, and tomorrow, being Good Friday, the fish fries will begin to fly off the shelves, or at least over the counters, which means no meat for all the good Catholics."

"Praise the Lord, Sam."

"Praise the Lord, Dan. This company already is getting free advertising on the front page of a national newspaper."

I had piqued Sam's curiosity and wasn't about to let it go. I looked at him and I asked if he thought there was any chance that the Pope might actually endorse a fish sandwich and what he might be able to charge.

Sam was laughing.

"So what do you think, Sam, maybe free sandwiches for him and his cronies for the duration of the Lenten season?"

Sam smiled and replied, "I don't think the Pope is for sale, but maybe a fishbowl on wheels with a guy in a pointy hat going through the drive-up window would result in a Kodak moment. It would have the same result and you wouldn't even have to say it was him."

"Sam, I have one even better. The drive-through window could have a crackly speaker with a serious sounding voice on the other side saying, "And just what brings you, my child. I am here to listen not only to your past sins, but to take your order. Sam, it would be like the confessional of our youth. The person driving through could confess:

"'Bless me, father, for I have sinned. I have lusted after a ham sandwich. This is my one and only sin. I would like three fish sandwiches, three sides of unleavened fries, a glass of wine and two sodas and if you could throw a little Holy Water on my kids in the back, that would be nice."

"'God bless you, my child. That will be twelve dollars and sixty-seven cents, as well as two Hail Mary's and an Our Father and may the peace of the Lord be with you.'"

Sam piped up, "And also with you, Dan, but seriously, whether or not the Pope gives his blessing, it has already worked."

He was always thinking with his corporate mind, and I always responded with my wiseass comments. It was fun for us both.

I had heated up the pancakes that had gotten cold and fried a couple of eggs and brought out a little honey to drizzle on top.

"Sam, I know it ain't no Yellow Jack. The truth is that fish was just a little okay. Do me a favor out of your respect for our friendship and believe that. Don't ask Linda or Latona their thoughts. They probably wouldn't want to hurt my feelings and would be polite telling you just how delicious they thought it was."

The sight of those pancakes in front of him was enough to make him forget. He exclaimed how wonderful they were.

I said that I would be doing a little grocery shopping later that day and if he needed anything, or wanted to go with me, to let me know.

"Dan, I would love to come along. I need to stock up on a few supplies. What store are you going to?"

I told him that I had no preferences and he said that there was a grocery store in Marathon that had the best chicken salad.

"Marathon it is, Sam."

He was tired and said he'd be napping for a little while. I told him when he got his lazy ass up to come find me.

I sat at my site for a little while before heading to the showers and passed Sam as he was coming out. "I'll see you in a little while, Sam."

He said he just needed a little rest and wouldn't be too long.

A few hours, or however long, later I was sitting at my campsite with "BeBop," another camper, when Sam showed up.

BeBop looked at Sam and said, "Hey, Sam, I was just telling Dan how we used to be next door neighbors on the ocean and how I used to hear you raising a ruckus every morning." He said that Sam would be awake and making a lot of noise in his camper as early as 4:00 A.M.

"Dan, at first I thought he was just stumbling around, maybe even drunk, and when I asked him if everything was okay, he said that he was making coffee and it was just the pots and pans bouncing off each other."

BeBop smiled as he told the story, and I laughed. I told BeBop that Sam and I were heading into Marathon for some groceries if he needed anything, or he could come along as well if he'd like.

He declined and left, I suppose heading off to another site to visit other friends for a little while before moving on to the next.

I asked Sam and asked if he was ready to shop, and he was. "Well then, Mr. Catalano... your chariot awaits."

We got into my truck and off we went to the "big city" of Marathon. In actuality, it did have a lot of businesses along the main road and probably beyond and I do believe it was considered a city.

Sam told me that the Publix food store had the best chicken salad he had ever had. I already knew Sam well enough to know it was probably at least good.

"Dan, I like keeping simple foods on hand and a container of food already prepared. That makes it easier for me to eat when I'm hungry. Their chicken salad is always in my refrigerator when I need something to eat."

I dropped him and his groceries off at his site and proceeded on to mine. He took a nap and it wasn't too long after that he stopped by and told me that Jonie was having dinner that evening and that I was expected to be there as well.

I looked at him. "Am I to assume that I am to be your date for this event, and if so what is the proper attire? Are we now perceived among the campground as a couple?"

"Dan, don't take it personally, but even with your cute ass, you are not my type."

That evening Sam grabbed a bottle of wine and I grabbed a can of popcorn, and we walked over to Jonie's where the food and company were both entertaining. She had invited the Pirates as well. They refused to grow up and were down here, being well known amongst the campground for their antics.

There was a Chuck (Captain Cutie), another Chuck (One-eyed), a Bill (a.k.a. Horny Bill), and John. Any woman walking by was fair game for their catcalls, whistles, and remarks of her beauty. Many in Electric wouldn't even venture past their domain, although in observing those that did (at least the women), few didn't smile and wiggle their fanny just a little more as they went by. I think it was the husbands that didn't like the Pirates.

After a few cocktails and the food consumed, it seemed as though I was the one placed on the grill. Sam told everyone how I had betrayed him the previous night, selling my soul for a few pieces of fish.

The Pirates all jumped on board.

"He's a Judas, I'm a tellin' ya."

Everyone chimed in and I told them all that the cock hadn't crowed three times in a row in more than a couple of years, at least not mine. I started calling them "those crusty old blue-balled biker bastards from Wisconsin."

The more rum that was consumed, the more harassment I received, and I did my best to give it back, though I do believe they got the best of me. It was a fun night and I had somehow managed to survive their onslaught.

Sam and I stumbled back to his place arm in arm. I am sure it was like Sam's gait one step forward, two to the side, and one back, though in tandem, and I guess I somehow managed to make it back to mine.

Chapter 13

Mourning Has Broken

The sun was just beginning to brighten the horizon and to fade the stars. I was sitting outside amongst some of the most beautiful things on this planet: campers and nature. Blackbirds were singing their songs as well.

Along came Sam, and as he entered my campsite, not only did the horizon brighten, but my day began to as well. Sam was always a ray of sunshine to anyone that knew him.

"Good morning, buddy."

It was all he said. It made me smile and I knew that today was going to be a good day. Every day was a good day when it started with a cup of coffee and a side order of Sam.

He sat down across from me. As we drank our first morning's cup of coffee together, I thought that if there truly was karma in this world, then I must have done something good in either this life or in a past one, and I was being rewarded with a peace and tranquility beyond what I normally experienced in my day-to-day life. I really couldn't imagine what I could possibly have done right, at least not in this life.

A pair of mourning doves were perched in the trees above my campsite, cooing to each other their forlorn-sounding song.

I looked at Sam and asked, "Why do those birds sound so sad? Are they mourning the fact that they mate for life?"

Sam gave me a look that seemed both disappointed and amused, and I knew he was about to explain the obvious, or more likely tell me just a bunch of crap.

"No, Dan, those are not mourning doves. They are actually referred to by most people as 'happy birds of the morning.' They usually travel in pairs, a male and female together. Their song is normally quite joyful. Most people, and even a few scientists, proclaim that they are expressing their love for one another. It's usually quite happy and expressive. The only thing that I can think of that would make them sound so sad is that your ugly ass is beneath them and they are not at all pleased with that."

"Sam, I am beginning to think that I must have done something wrong in this or a past life that I am now being punished with you as a friend. Karma is a bitch, and I think that it's coming back to bite me in my ass through you."

Normally it took us about two sips of coffee before conversation began. We would talk about nothing and everything almost as if we had known each other a lifetime. Since my twenties, I had not experienced taking the time to enjoy people and life and take in my surroundings. I was now at a time and place in my life that I was willing and able to get away for a little while to relax. Sam was at a place in his life where he was happy to be alive and do what he loved most: enjoy the company of others and exchange stories and thoughts.

He had already been to the newspaper box in front of campground's store and had his copy of *USA Today*. We sat there reading it, he with the business section and I with the sports section.

I was reading an article about Tiger Woods. What a surprise that he should be in the papers. I peered over my paper and said to Sam, "Hey, what do you think of this Eldrick Woods guy. I myself personally kinda like him."

Sam looked at me and his face kind of scrunched up. "Who the hell is Eldrick Woods?"

I told him Eldrick was Tiger Woods' birth name.

Sam set down his paper and his face lit up. "What? Are you kidding me? I LOVE Tiger Woods!"

Sam was ecstatic as he continued. "Dan, ever since that fucking movie came out, *A River Runs Through It*, every yuppie, every preppie, or every wannabe fisherman suddenly found themselves going through their catalogues and buying whatever they thought was the proper attire for a fly fisherman."

Sam almost seemed angry when remembering. "I have to think that L. L. Bean sales people had to call these fools their 'catch of the day.' They hit the rivers and streams in their full regalia: the proper hat, the right vest, the most expensive rod they could find. They would appear on the rivers in droves, showing off their brand-new attire, trying to cast a fly, as if they were repeating the last video they saw on how to fly fish. They waded into the waters wearing their boots, trying to seem as if they knew what they were doing, and it made me sad. The solitude of the river was suddenly gone. They ruined everything I loved about fly fishing. I used to try to outwit the fish, and I found myself trying to outsmart those idiots for a little space on the rivers."

Sam's expression softened and he almost looked happy as he continued, "Well, along came Tiger Woods and they put away their fly rods and hip waders and returned to the stores after having read the articles telling them about the proper equipment for their latest endeavors. They replaced fly rods with golf clubs, waders with khakis, flies with balls, a hat that shaded them with a baseball cap that had a logo on it.

"They left the rivers and streams and found the greens. When they invaded my sanctuary, I used to think, *not on MY fucking river*!

"GOD, I *love* Tiger Woods! The rivers are again serene. It's a place that I think maybe there is a God, or at least a place where I can commune with Nature or my own soul. I really don't know. I just know that the rivers are again at peace with those who love Her."

It was fun to watch how thrilled Sam became over what had started out as just another topic of discussion. Whether it was his nature or his disease that left him so open with his feelings I don't know, though I think that Sam was always open with his heart.

I told him of my mother, who at the age of ninety enjoyed watching golf on TV. Before Tiger came along, she used to question her sister's sanity for wasting an afternoon sitting around watching a golf tournament.

"Well, along came Tiger Woods, and he changed all that. If he is on TV, my mother is watching. She even looks over the sports section, hoping for an article about him. He is, for whatever a reason, a person people are drawn to, though to give my mom credit, she was never really a threat to your precious rivers."

Sam was one of those people that I would describe as a sportsman. His quarry had to be a challenge, one that required both skill and patience, an adversary that had to be learned and studied in order to take luck somewhat out of the equation in order to catch with any kind of frequency. I, on the other hand, was more of a meat hunter with a fishing pole. I was looking for something to throw into the frying pan.

I would describe my fishing style as like an old black person on the bank of a lake or creek, maybe sitting on a dock with a bamboo pole with a cork and a worm on the end, not looking for bragging rights, just looking to enjoy the day and to get a meal at the end of it all.

I really cannot relate to Sam and so many others who, like him, had the philosophy of catch and release, those that were more about outsmarting their prey as opposed to those, like me, who wanted to eat them. I was more catch and fillet, a meal more than a memory. A fish caught worth bragging about was more an accident than by design.

Sitting there, I asked Sam if he was hungry. He wanted to go out to a restaurant, and he would be buying.

I pulled out my frying pan and some bacon and eggs and told Sam to bite my ass. I was going to cook.

Another camper stopped by and Sam began with his introductions. I think he knew everyone in this place who had been here before.

I extended my hand. "Hi, Ron from Minnesota, I'm Dan from New York." We had met the previous year. I told Ron to have a seat and grabbed a coffee mug and poured him a cup. I was in the process of cooking and was adding a little for him. He declined and thanked me for the offer.

Sam and Ron began talking of the time when Ron and his son had visited Sam at his summer retreat in Montana, on the Big Horn River at a campground renowned for its trout fishing.

Sam was talking of how much he loved Minnesota, because every town, no matter how small, had at least one Dairy Queen, and Dairy Queen had Blizzards, and there is nothing better than a Blizzard.

Ron told me that Blizzards were nothing more than Dairy Queen's version of a vanilla milkshake, but Sam yelled out, "No they're not! They are the nectar of the gods!"

Ron's trip was not that long ago and he told me how he was amazed that, even with the advancement of Sam's disease, Sam was able to take his fly rod and place a fly where he wanted to almost every time.

Sam, of course, told Ron he was "full of shit" and that he could barely find the water.

"Dan, knowing the way Sam is now, and even then, if I hadn't seen it, I wouldn't have believed it."

In the little time I'd known Sam, I knew it to be true. Even though Huntington's was laying claim to his body, he had such a strong will and focused mind that he commanded his body to do what his disease tried to deny him.

"Dan, the first time we went out to the river to fish, Sam broke his fly rod and he was so pissed he actually punched me in the arm and said, 'That fries my apples.' I looked at my son and we had no idea what that meant, and after Sam calmed down he went on to explain that he'd said, 'that fries my ass' (Sam's words were sometimes affected by his disease as well). Now, anytime me or my son gets mad we say, 'that fries my apples.'"

Sam said he'd broken poles before, and I suppose he was frustrated that he couldn't control certain things anymore. It was a testament to their friendship that Sam punched him, and Ron laughed about it.

Sam had his exercise class to go to, and Ron was making the social rounds, so we parted ways. The skies were threatening rain. The wind was blowing pretty hard and I figured to give the fish the day off.

Bill (Horny Bill) was riding his bicycle and stopped in. When I asked him what he was doing that day, he responded the way so many others that resided here did, "Well, I'm thinking that I might get my tire fixed on my bicycle. It's been losing air." A week later, I asked Bill what he was up to that day and his response was the same. Bill still had not fixed his tire. He just took a few more trips up front to add air to that tire.

And that, folks, is the camping lifestyle of many a people here. When it comes to what someone is doing, the response is often the same... "Well, I'm thinking that maybe..."And the next day there was a pretty good chance that they were still thinking of maybe doing the same. It's a wonderful lifestyle that takes all of a couple days to arrive at that same mentality.

I did my dishes from that morning and from the night before. It was noon before I actually got off my ass. I headed up front to the Laundromat with a load of clothes.

I crossed paths with Sam as he too was heading up front. When I told him that I was doing my laundry, he looked at me and said quite seriously, "Dan, you'd better be careful up there."

Clothes having been put in the washing machine, I went over to the Liars' Bench, a place outside the store where people gathered and told stories. A few people were there, Sam being one of them. He was sitting with Judy and a few others from the campground. I sat down next to them for a few minutes and we discussed politics, religion, and the current state of the economy as well as the various idiosyncrasies of those that camped. In other words, we shot the shit for a little bit.

I had to get back to the Laundromat to check on my clothes, and Sam again told me to be careful. "Dan, the last time I did my own laundry up there I made the mistake of taking up three machines and I almost came to blows with someone that thought I should only be using two. It was to the point where I was ready to throw punches. It was really scary. I think she would have kicked my ass if I hadn't backed down. Those women can be mean up there."

I knew what he meant. There is something about that Laundromat that brings out people's true nature. Clothes in a machine left unattended after its cycle had completed, sometimes for even as little as a minute, could wind up in a pile on the table. I guess some people are on a tight schedule and have someplace to go or something to do, but I never was told of anything anyone was going to do that couldn't wait. To be fair to the impatient assholes, there are only five or six washers, and the same for dryers, for the whole campground (though for most it's enough).

"Sam, the last time I did laundry there, I was up at the pool (above the Laundromat) and (a different) Judy was below and I called to her and asked if she would put a couple of quarters in the dryer to keep it going. She told me that it was the time of women's liberation and declined. I asked her, if that was the case, why George (her boyfriend) was back at their place drinking a beer while she was doing the laundry. All she said was, 'touché' as she walked away. Another time I asked someone who was folding his laundry if he needed a hand, as he was folding his sheets. He called me a son of a bitch, saying that was his boxer shorts."

I said my goodbyes and made it to the machines before they'd reached their deadline and switched my clothes to the dryer, avoiding any confrontation. Waiting for the dryers to do their thing, I sat just outside (on guard) reading an article in *Cosmopolitan* about finding my "G" spot. I still don't get it.

That day I socialized; that night I slept.

Chapter 14

I Want to Ride My Bicycle

The sun was peeking over the trees and Sam was peeking around the corner as he was a roundin' the bend heading into my campsite. Sam had his newspaper in one hand and his non-spill coffee cup in the other.

I told Sam that he needed a little more beauty sleep, and he told me that even if I slept like Rip Van Winkle it probably wouldn't be enough sleep to help me.

We both smiled, and I filled his cup with coffee, and we both exclaimed what a glorious morning it was. It was warm enough if you wanted to wear shorts and T-shirt and cool enough for pants and long-sleeved tops.

When you're from a cold winter climate and the threat of snow is always a constant, it is so nice to be in a place that experiences seventy degrees almost every day. Rain or shine, it beats the hell out of a cold, dreary day back up north. In South Florida the sun is much more a constant than the clouds; back home the clouds are much more of a constant than the sun, at least in the winter. Even the occasional downpour of rain that leaves you walking through puddles beats the hell out of snow. You don't have to shovel rain.

Sam's body was moving about more than normal. "Sam, what's going on? You seem more nervous than a long-tailed cat—"

"In a room full of rocking chairs?" he finished before I could. "Dan, I thought you were a little more original than that."

I didn't respond right away. "Sam, I like to think I am, and if you would allow me to complete a sentence before you finish it for me, you might be rewarded with an original thought. I was about to say that you seem more nervous than a long-tailed cat at a clown convention."

He thought about that one for a second or two, or maybe three, then let out his loud "*HA!*" "Very good, Dan, It took me a second to get it."

Sam had the same mentality as me. I don't know if that was a good thing for others, but it worked for me.

Before I could finish asking what was bothering him, he asked, "Dan, what do you know about bicycles?"

"Sam, I do have a little bit of mechanical know-how, and bicycles are right up there at the top of that list. You see, it seems as though when you push down on a pedal with one foot that the other pedal rises to the top. You then push down on that with the other foot and the other pedal comes back up and it somehow propels the bicycle into a forward motion. It is truly a marvel to the ingenuity of mankind. Who'd a thunk that pushing a foot down could propel a vehicle forward?"

Sam knew me enough to ignore my sarcastic remarks. "Dan, the gearshift on my bicycle broke apart and it ended up scattered all over the ground. I think I've found all the pieces, but I'm not really sure. The parts fell into the coral. I had a pretty tough time even finding a few parts."

Since Sam's bicycle was his means to get around the campground, the thought of not having his campground transport was bothering him. He was at a loss as to what to do.

Sam liked to have his life in order as much as he could. Anything that disrupted that order left him a little flustered. Anytime he lost a little control, he was that much closer to having no control.

"Sam, let's have some coffee and something to eat, and I'll see if we can figure it out."

He went back to his campsite and returned with a bag of nuts, bolts, and a spring, as well as his bicycle. I examined the parts and the gearshift that they came from. The whole while, Sam paced, trying to contain himself. His head as well as his arms moved about more than usual.

His mind kept him somewhat in control of his disease, which made what might be a simple problem to most others such a big deal to him.

I looked up at him. "I really do not think this should be too much of a problem... (He looked really relieved as I continued.) ...for a bike shop. I have absolutely positively no fucking idea how this thing goes back together."

"Dan, there's a bike shop up the road. Do you think we could put my bike in your truck and go there? I'll buy you breakfast."

"Sam, with an offer like that, how could I possibly refuse? Not only that, but I would hate to think that your beautiful fanny would not be parading around this campground on your bicycle any longer. You are doing me, as well as the rest of the people here, a favor."

I loaded his bike and his bag of parts into my truck and proceeded to the bike shop no more than a mile down the road.

The name of the place was Big Pine Key Bike Shop. We walked into the store and an employee told us that he would be right with us, that he just had to make the final adjustments on a bike someone was buying.

Sam informed me that the employee was actually the owner. While waiting for him to complete his sale, we unloaded Sam's bike and brought it to the front of the store. The previous customer taken care of, he turned his attention to Sam. He extended his hand and asked him how he was doing.

Sam let out a loud "GOOD. I am doing good, Marty."

"And what can I do for you today, Sam?"

Sam handed him the bag of parts, explaining the problem, with the owner examining the various components.

"Let me grab some tools and we'll see just what we have here."

Marty returned with a few tools. "I've never had one of this particular type of shifter apart before. These things never seem to have a problem."

He would take all the parts and put them together only to have them fall apart while turning the final screw. After several attempts, he looked up with an expression that I couldn't read.

"This screw has a reverse thread! Just the opposite of anything I would have expected."

After a few more attempts and the parts jumping apart, the shifter was back together. He looked at Sam. "I think we've got it, Sam. How does five dollars sound?"

Sam responded, "Ten sounds better," and handed him the money.

"Thanks."

It had taken the owner more than a few minutes to figure out the problem, and Sam knew his time was worth more than five dollars. He also knew that those he dealt with liked him, and he did not want to feel that he was a charity case.

With his condition, he had to rely on others to some degree. Between that and his personality, people remembered him, and he was not about to take advantage of the bonds he had formed.

I walked Sam's bike to the back of my truck and he stopped me. "Dan, I have to take it for a ride to make sure it's working okay."

A part of Sam's analytical mind was making sure everything was in order, making sure that he was comfortable with the results.

Off he went down the road, his head bobbing and his body moving about, but the bicycle still maintained its direction, never swaying from the path he chose for it. His body might have been a little off kilter, but his bike went straight.

Though I was concerned for Sam on a main road with traffic, I was not about to express my thoughts. He was a big boy who, against all odds, was still maintaining a life on his own.

I was in awe of the guy.

He returned to the parking lot satisfied that his bike was the same as before his nuts and bolts fell apart. As I loaded his bike into the back of my truck, he walked back toward the shop opening the door and yelled out, "Thank you!"

The owner yelled back, "My pleasure, Sam! Thank you!"

We climbed into my truck and proceeded on down the road for our morning's breakfast.

Though I suspected that I already knew the answer, I still asked, "I am curious why you wouldn't buy a three-wheel bicycle. I would think it would be a whole lot easier?"

Sam looked off into the distance. "Dan, I have to push myself. The reason I don't have a three-wheel bike is the same reason I don't have a handicap sticker. I can't take the easy way. It's what keeps me going. I have to push myself, and if I didn't, it would be to accept defeat."

I told Sam that I was amazed at how often those in our society that had handicap stickers were the ones that needed them the least. Doctors hand out those stickers even while saying to exercise.

"Sam, now that I think about it, what you are telling me is you are just a bullheaded son of a bitch."

Sam feigned being insulted and continued, "Not only that, Dan, but I bought this bike for twenty bucks, and those three-wheelers are expensive!"

"Okay, Sam, you are not only a bullheaded S.O.B., you are a cheap bastard!"

"I prefer to think of myself as frugal and determined."

I mumbled, "cheap and hardheaded," as we continued on our way for a breakfast at the restaurant of Sam's choosing.

We pulled into the parking lot. I asked Sam if he had a lock for his bicycle so we could secure it to my truck.

"Yes I do, Dan."

We parked and Sam went into the bag on the front of his bike and produced a lock and chain and tried to open it. He thought he knew the combination, but all his attempts at opening it failed. He told me the numbers and I tried with the same results.

I changed spots to a parking space next to a privacy fence along the outdoor seating section of the restaurant, though the holes, gaps, and missing sections allowed very little privacy.

"Sam, I think your bike is safe. We'll sit inside along the fence and be able to see your twenty-dollar investment. If anyone goes for it, you'll be able to push right through this barrier and tackle them while I call the police."

Sam was appeased to some degree and we went inside to get a seat with my truck and his bike in our view. He said that he needed to buy a new lock.

"Sam why do even need a lock down here? I mean, how often do you even use it?"

"NEVER!" Although he went on to list all the different scenarios where he might need it, whether it being a trip to the flea market (never) or riding around Key West (again never happening) or to places that we both knew were just hopes.

We ordered our breakfast and sat there eating while I told him his real problem. "You do realize what is happening?" He looked at me and I continued, "I believe the scientific, or medical, term is a brain fart. It's really quite common and ain't no big deal. It happens a bit more frequently as we grow older. You'll remember the combination long before you'll ever need that lock."

His back was to the restaurant so he could see his bicycle, and when the waitress arrived, I held out my hand for the bill.

She smiled at me and handed it to Sam.

"Sam, you son of a bitch! You're only willing to spend twenty dollars on a bike yet you'll spend twenty bucks on a meal that I wanted to buy. All right, Sam. You've proved you're at least bullheaded."

We left the restaurant and were heading back to camp when Sam said that he wanted to stop back at the bike shop.

"What for, Sam? You haven't even ridden your bicycle yet. What the hell can be wrong with it?"

He wanted to buy a lock, so his bike wouldn't be stolen.

"Sam, that shop has to get ten to twenty dollars for a lock. We can probably get one for five bucks at the flea market."

He wanted a lock from the bike shop. "Dan, they take care of me and I'll take care of them."

Sam was a class act. He went inside and returned with a lock that he would probably never use, but his mind was a little more at ease for the time being.

I asked him if he remembered to get the combination. He never bothered to respond.

"I hope you told the owner to keep a record of it in your file."

We returned to the camp and Sam immediately jumped on his bike to take it for a ride.

I decided that I needed to catch a few fish. After buying some frozen bait from the store up front, I headed out onto the seas.

Later that day Sam stopped by and told me that we had been invited out to dinner that evening with a few other people, those being Minnesota Ron, little Jonie along with her companion Jack, Sam, and myself.

The restaurant was named Rob's and the place was full. Sam said that when he first came down here he would frequent this place as many as three times a week.

"Dan, those that ran this place got to know me, and after a while they would have a guy whose only job when I was here was to follow me

-152-

around. I sometimes drop things, and this guy would pick up after me and make sure I was okay. Anyone who didn't know me thought I was a staggering drunk. He made sure that I had no problems. He tried to be discreet, but I knew. One time I pulled him aside and threw him twenty dollars and said, 'Thanks.' After that, he kind of hung around me and smiled, and we both pretended to not know what he was actually doing."

We ordered our food, and Jack, who seemed more than a little arrogant, was talking about how he had just sold his sailboat and was going to take that money and see the world. He was a tall man, at least in relation to Jonie, who was maybe four-foot-six on a good day. He was maybe four-foot-eight standing up straight and on his tippy toes.

We ate our meal. Sam and I went outside and smoked a cigarette. Upon our return, the little man had already paid the bill. When I asked what I owed him, he said that the dinner was on him.

I told him, "Thanks but no. Everyone else here is your friend and I am just a tagalong. You didn't sell your boat so you could blow it on strangers."

He tried to argue, but when I threw him twenty bucks and said, "Besides, you seem to be a little short." He took my money without another word.

Back at the campground Sam asked what I had thought of him. I said that I felt he was suffering from a Napoleon complex. He was a little rude to the waitresses and his stature left him with an attitude that tried to compensate.

Sam didn't disagree. "Dan, he's normally really a nice guy, and believe it or not, I think he was trying to impress you."

I told him that I couldn't imagine why anyone would want to impress me and he agreed. Regardless of the big man's attitude, it had been a good day.

Chapter 15

The Duke/College

The next morning I was awake, though still lying in bed, when I heard a vaguely familiar voice from my past.

"Oh, Danny."

Okay maybe the vaguely familiar voice was Sam and the past was just yesterday, but it was still only vaguely that I heard him, and yesterday was the past after all.

"Good morning, Sam."

"Dan, I hope I'm not waking you. It's such a beautiful day that I would have really felt guilty if I let you waste it away lying inside a camper sleeping."

"No, Sam, I was already awake and I really do appreciate your concern, even though I think that you, sir, are full of shit. You are just looking for a cup of the best coffee south of the Mississippi."

"Dan, the only thing south of the Mississippi is the Gulf of Mexico."

"That and me Sam, I'm a bit to the south."

I told him coffee would be a few minutes and he immediately said that he wanted to go out for breakfast to another place that he liked.

"Dan, are you going fishing today?"

"You betcha, Sam, though I will let you buy me breakfast *if and only if* you let me cook some fish tonight."

I guess that he had an opening on his schedule for his evening meal and agreed to my invitation. It seemed that almost every night he was invited to someone's place, and I guessed that no one had yet filled his slate for this evening.

I poured us both a cup of coffee.

I wear T-shirts and have coffee mugs that have something to say. On this particular day, my coffee cup had the words, "Stolen from the bedroom of John Wayne."

Sam took one look at it and then a look at me. "I knew it!"

I looked at him. "You knew it, Sam? If you knew it, then I think that would mean that you used to know something. To 'knew' is to have known something and that would be the past tense of knowing. So I can only assume that you used to know something then forgot it? Are you now remembering it? Or are you just upset with knewing something and now not knowing?"

Sam ignored me and continued pointing at my coffee cup. "Your mug is from the bedroom of John Wayne."

"Yes, Sam, the coffee cup says 'stolen from the bedroom of John Wayne,' and just what is your point?"

"Dan, the point is I knew you only wanted me for my body. You are gay!"

I looked at him, trying to seem as though his statement came as a shock. "Oh no, Sam, please don't tell me it's true!

"I'm GAY? Well, why the hell didn't anyone tell me before now! I had no idea, and to think all this time I've been wasting my virility with women, thinking that I was enjoying everything about them!

"Oh my God, Sam, I really had no idea! Sam, give me a break, cut me just a little bit of slack here. We are talking the Duke after all, and it was only one time.

"I was born in this country and a native to it, yet the only place I am called an American is any place else in the world. In the land of my ancestors, Germany, I am an 'American.' Yet here in this country I am referred to as a German. No one calls me a native.

"I wired my own house for electricity. Does anyone call me an electrician? No!

"I put a roof on my house, though no one has ever called me a roofer.

"I fix my own vehicles. No one says I'm a mechanic.

"But suck just one little cock, one time, and the rest of your life everyone refers to you as *that cocksucker*!

"You, sir, are being way too judgmental, and I am hurt. I was young, Sam, and it really was only the one time."

"Just the one time, Dan?"

"Only once, Sam. Sorry if I am letting you down. I hope you're not too awfully disappointed. I am straight."

Sam said he remembered his first "blow job," and when I asked about what he thought of the taste, he just let out a laugh and said no more.

Mr. Mike was making his way up to the front store and stopped by. He and his son Bruce had been coming down here from Connecticut for six weeks every year for many years. Mike (I called him Mr. Mike) was ninety years old and a fisherman like I was, out for the fun and hopefully a meal. His son had gotten his love of both fishing and hunting from his father, and I suppose he was reciprocating what he had received in his childhood, a selfless devotion that most of us do not truly take the time to appreciate returning in kind to those that gave us so much.

The winds were blowing that day and the seas were a bit rough. Mr. Mike was staying on land. At ninety years old, his sea legs weren't what they used to be. Sunshine and people were better than bruised legs and being tossed around in a boat.

He would stop and visit people, or rest on a bench, while walking about the campground. Oftentimes he'd go fishing with Bruce, though the seas dictated whether he'd be on land or the ocean.

Mr. Mike went on his way and Sam started bellyaching that he was hungry and was ready to eat. I told him that I was heading to the showers and would see him in a few. He went on back to his campsite.

Shortly thereafter, I returned to Sam's with my truck. "C'mon Sam, let's go."

He got in and we headed out to the restaurant of his choice. The place we'd previously found lots of places to park seemed to be full. Maybe it was because they were open today. We parked on the side and headed into the restaurant, sitting in the outside section where smoking was allowed.

"Sam, I hope the only reason that you wanted to come here isn't just because they have a smoking section."

He assured me the food was good, and I asked him why he still smoked. (I was a smoker as well.)

"It relaxes me, Dan. When I sat with my doctor and we knew I had this disease, I asked him straight out if I should quit. He said there was no reason to. I guess it was then that I really knew I was fucked."

The way Sam said it was not to evoke sympathy from me or to feel sorry for himself. He stated it as a matter of fact. If his doctor proclaimed there was no reason to quit smoking, Sam realized he already had a death sentence from Huntington's and it would take him long before the damage caused by smoking would.

Since he was old enough to comprehend, Sam knew what his fate might be. I've no idea how long it took him to come to terms with his fate once it was acknowledged, though I've a feeling that he just accepted it and moved on to embrace the life he had.

Huntington's is hereditary. If a parent has it, there is a chance that their children might as well, and Sam had watched it progress through his mother. He knew if he had that same gene, just what lay ahead for him. It was only a possibility, but if inherited, it is a death sentence.

We ordered our food, and conversation found its way into Sam's college years.

"So, Sam, you went to the University of Michigan?"

"No, I went to Michigan *State* University, and it was wonderful. You know that before college I had never even gotten laid."

"You gotta be shittin' me, Sam. Are you trying to tell me that you didn't even discover what your penis was for before college?"

Sam looked at me almost as if he was insulted by my question.

"No, Dan, I discovered it long before that, but I suppose I was having so much fun with it myself that I guess I just didn't want to share it with anyone else. I am totally serious. It might not have even been till my second year of college before I had been with a woman."

From the first time I met Sam I liked him. I also admired him for how honest he was. Every story he shared seemed to be just a matter of fact. Most men would not readily admit to going through high school, let alone well into college, still a virgin. With Sam, every story was a reflection on how things really were in his life.

"When I went to college, it was the sixties and women were finally becoming both comfortable with their own sexuality and quite open with it. It was before the progression of AIDS and after the advent of the pill. God, it was such a wonderful time. Women had been repressed since the beginning of time and they were only too happy to make up for the generations that had been denied any freedom before them.

"Women were burning their bras, and men were throwing away their rubbers. The Vietnam War was in full swing, and after college, us guys might very well be sent off to die. We really believed that, and we were enjoying everything that life had to offer before that happened.

"If you went out on a date with someone, it was pretty much accepted that you would spend the night together. It was just accepted by both, *and* to top all that off, I was in charge of the girls' dorm. Once word got out among them that I was fun and never spoke of anything that happened, I was almost passed around."

"Sam, you are telling me that basically you were a slut."

"Young and dumb, Dan, young and dumb. I was not only getting an education from books, but in life. It was the sixties after all, and who was I to deny these women that which was held back from them by society since the beginning of time. I was only a cog in the gear that would have moved forth even without my help."

Not to be outdone with Sam's education, I told him that I'd lost my virginity in high school. "And, you know what, Sam? We were not taught promiscuity. I, sir, am not a slut."

I told him of my first experience long before my college years, in the loft of a garage, with my childhood sweetheart and my first wife. (Hell it could have been last week, since I never went to college.) I was young and dumb as well, though I did not have the wisdom to disassociate love and sex. In actuality I guess I'm still a bit confused about them both.

"Dan, I remember back in college a friend of mine telling me probably the most honest thing I've ever heard someone say. It was during the Vietnam War and most of us were worried, and yet he joined the Marines. When I asked him why, he said that he would probably never again have a chance to kill someone."

I said that a friend of mine that was a very successful lawyer told me that, in essence, "I get paid to lie." And I found that pretty honest, though paling in comparison to what Sam had just said.

Sam mentioned another friend who they nicknamed "P" brain. "Dan, during college we'd go out to a bar and he would start at the top, hitting on the most beautiful woman there and would go on to the next till he found someone willing to go home with him.

"He's now a father and there was this one time this kid came over to take his daughter out on a date. He took one look at what he was driving, a van, and asked him if he'd ever driven a Mercedes as he tossed him the keys. Knowing the way *he'd* been, he wasn't about to let his daughter go out in a 'hotel room on wheels.'"

We smoked our cigarettes, drank our coffee, and ate our breakfast. I had nodded at the waitress upon our arrival, rubbing my fingers together as if I was holding money and assumed she understood that the bill was to be mine, but she knew Sam, and he somehow had arranged that he would be buying.

I was beginning to see just how greedy a person Sam was to go so far as denying me such a simple thing in life like paying for a meal in a restaurant.

"Sam, you really are an asshole."

"Dan, what can I say, you make good coffee and you're kinda cute. I'm trying to get on your good side."

"Piss off, Sam."

We left the restaurant and headed back to camp, he to sleep and me to fish. I dropped him off at his place, and I got some frozen shrimp from the front store, grabbed my fishing poles, jumped into my boat, and went out onto the ocean to catch a meal and enjoy the day.

Sam slept.

I fished.

I returned to camp with a smile on my face and fish in the cooler, not only enough fish for that night's meal but a few for the freezer for when I returned home.

I had told Sam to stop by whenever, and it wasn't long after I got back to my place that he did. He brought some beer and we sat and continued our foray into our pasts.

I come into contact with so many people in my life, though I never take the time to really get to know them. I realize how pathetic that is. I also know it's the choice that so many of us make, to deal with people rather than get to know them.

After a few beers and more than a few stories exchanged, I fired up the charcoal grill. That day I had caught some Cero Mackerel. They were not only fun to catch but wonderful to eat when cooked with a little Cajun seasoning. A baked potato and some rice would complement that fish.

I served Sam his meal and afterwards he began to praise my genius in cooking. "I'm serious, Dan, that fish was wonderful."

"Sam, I know you're just blowing smoke up my ass because you like to eat, though it's okay. I do like to cook."

He told me of a couple of recipes he had in his camper that he wanted me to have, one for Rosetta and one for lamb. "I'll see if I can't find them and give them to you."

"Sam, they are probably sitting along with that article you wrote about hunting with dogs." He told me that he would find that as well.

A few more beers and he was ready for some sleep. He headed back to his home; I went into my camper with my notes and continued my writing.

Chapter 16

Curley and the Panty Sniffer

The next morning, after talking over a few cups of coffee, or a pot or two, Sam and I decided to go up front for a copy of *USA today*.

We both poured ourselves a cup of the camp's brew from the store and went outside to the Liars' Bench to rub elbows with our fellow socialites: the derelicts with their tents, and the millionaires, some with their hundred-thousand-dollar motor homes. For anyone new here, it was hard to tell one from the other.

This wonderful gathering place was a way to kickstart the day for a lot of campers. More than a few people had gathered around, Larry—someone I'd come to know and like—being one of them. He stood up and said he was hungry and that he was going to host breakfast at his place. He invited a few of us to join him and we decided who'd bring what.

Larry had brought some Portuguese Chorizo with him from wherever he was from, someplace in the Northeast, I think. He mixed it with some eggs and a few other secret ingredients. With that, along with some bacon, bowls of fruit, toast, juices, and fried potatoes, we had a wonderful meal.

If I were to describe Larry (and I guess I am), I'd say he was a tall man, maybe five feet eight inches. I say he was tall is because he was at least a little taller than his hair, which he'd apparently outgrown. (Larry did not have much hair.) His head had shot right up and through his golden locks, leaving behind no more than a fringe under the tanned globe of his dome. He was an affable character, always smiling and ready to enjoy everyone he came into contact with. If it was after twelve, he'd have a beer in his hand. He'd look at his watch every morning, counting away the minutes till noon. Larry was on vacation after all.

I didn't waste any time to start messing with him. It really was his fault. I tend to mess with people I like, and when they tell me to piss off, I figure they like me as well. I liked Larry.

I asked everyone if anyone of them knew why Larry's eyes were red after sex, and none of them had a clue what I was talking about. Larry just looked at me.

Sam yelled out, "I KNOW! His eyes are red from the pepper spray!"

Larry was the only one who wasn't amused.

A few days prior, I'd lost my hairbrush, and I told Larry that with his lack of hair, I figured he probably didn't need his and I'd give him a good price for it, knowing that it had very few miles on it, if any.

Larry wasn't amused and started calling me "Demented Dan" to bust my chops. I let it go for a while. He seemed to be pretty proud of himself and kept on repeating it till I started calling him Curley.

It didn't take him long to decide he didn't like that name and called a truce.

I kinda liked calling a bald man Curley, yet I reluctantly agreed to his cease fire. "Larry, I will stop. I will get out of your hair!"

The talk amongst us got into politics and I asked Sam which party he adhered to. He said that he didn't follow a party. Afterwards he told me that he would vote for whatever party or candidate would be more likely to allow stem cell research. He felt that eventually there would be a breakthrough with his disease, and the only chance he had anytime soon was through stem cells. I think Sam was more of a Democrat and a liberal in his beliefs, but he didn't say it and I didn't I pursue it.

Ron was there along with his lovely wife Carol and he said in no uncertain terms that he was a Republican. I couldn't let that slide.

"And what religion, Ron?"

"I am a Catholic."

"Are your parents the same?"

"Yes."

I said that my parents were both Catholic and Republican as well and that I followed neither of those beliefs, much to my mother's chagrin. "Ron when I registered to vote, I didn't really know the difference in the political parties, so I just registered as an independent. I really can't understand why people follow their parents' beliefs without exploring other ideals and other beliefs, or other possibilities."

Ron was none too happy with my thoughts.

I think what really pissed him off was when I said, "We used to be a land of free thinkers. Our forefathers actually could no longer follow those that dictated 'their' desires and we became a free nation. Now we follow a 'party' that could not care any less about us. They take care of those that financially supported them, and both parties screw the masses. We're all a bunch of sheep blindly following our leaders so we can be slaughtered while the rich get richer and the poor get food stamps. I believe it's the Amish that want their children to go live in society for a year on their own before committing to their lifestyle. It used to be 'We the People' now it's the parties' agenda that most follow."

Oh well, I liked Ron. He really did seem like nice people and I figured I'd said enough. Ron was a big man. I have never been intimidated by a person's size, though I have over time come to the realization that "the bigger they are..." Well, it just seems that "...the harder they hit."

I am also learning (somewhat) to keep my mouth shut (sometimes) when it comes to religions and politics.

Lloyd and his wife of a whole bunch of years, Pam, were there as well. I started calling Lloyd, "Floyd," and after a few times, he tried correcting me. I explained that I was just shortening the name everyone else referred to him as: "That Fucking Lloyd." Hence, the shortened version "Floyd."

Lloyd was a big man as well. (Really big)

Conversation varied from politics to the weather, from religions to what people were going to do that day. It was a wonderful way to start the day, at least for me, getting under the skin of a few people and being able to get out of there while they were still not sure how to respond.

Campers can be a beautiful lot. I enjoy their diversity. How boring would life be if we all thought the same way, if we only talked with people of the same minds.

Sam and I walked back to his campsite. He'd gotten into the habit of putting his hand on my shoulder to help steady himself. He looked over at me. "You know, Dan, that I'm kind of feeling like Mike with his son Bruce. It seems like you are kind of taking care of me around here as well."

I said, "Piss off. You entertain me for now, and once I become bored with you, I'll just move on and you'll be left in my rearview mirror, if I even bother to look back at all."

Walking back, I told Sam not to tell anyone that, in the town I lived in, I liked the way things were run and thus far I had always voted across the board Republican.

"In that place, I do follow my parents' view of our town's future and the party that has led it to this point. Sam, I like my town and them damn Republicans that take care of it. We've even got an Italian as a supervisor, Mark Assini, that I hope sticks around, but he's almost too good insofar as his thoughts and work ethic, as well as his sincerity. If word gets out to others higher in the political arena, I am sure he'll move up the political ladder. He will get my vote, and anyone who is within hearing distance of my voice will know my thoughts on him."

I told Sam that I hope to never follow just one ideology, that I never become complacent with just one belief, whether it be religion or politics or even people, and I really had no desire to follow or to lead. "I just will find my own way I guess. The last person I voted for that I really liked was Ross Perot. I knew he didn't have a chance, but I hoped my vote might let people know something. I thought Obama was good, though he made me realize that good ideas weren't enough, that the Democrats and Republicans only cared about their own parties and not us. I think that maybe I just can't follow."

Back at Sam's campsite we sat down and I noticed for the first time the view Sam had from his site. He'd gone from one on the ocean that faced east and that every morning afforded him the opportunity to watch the sun as it rose above the ocean. He was an early riser. I am sure that he welcomed each and every new day as a blessing, and I have a feeling that the sun was wishing him a good morning as well.

Sitting there, I noticed someone on the staff of housekeeping cleaning the rails leading up to the facilities, a rather sweet girl with a pleasant disposition who always wore short cutoffs.

I looked at him. "Sam, you are a dog!"

He looked at me trying to look perplexed, but I knew better. We had both been looking at this girl bent over with the most beautiful fanny cheeks exposed just a little, and Sam looked at me and smiled.

"Sam, you ole turd. Here the whole time everyone thought you just needed to be closer to the restrooms. We all thought you moved to Electric to make you more comfortable. We all thought you were becoming a little lazy. You shit! Each and every woman in this campground (at least in Rustic) goes up and down those stairs every day, and you just sit here and watch! You, sir, are a just a horny bastard wanting to be closer to the action."

Sam looked at me and smiled. "Dan, I don't know if I'll ever again get laid."

When I asked him if his pecker just didn't work the same as when he was younger, he almost jumped out of his chair. "OF COURSE IT STILL WORKS!"

He continued, "And every time it gets hard, I beat it for all it's worth!"

I told Sam that "real" men don't masturbate, nor do they cry, and he responded that he cried whenever he didn't masturbate, and I said that I cried almost every time afterwards.

"Sam, I think that most women would love you. The way your body is always in motion it's almost as if you are a living, breathing vibrator. Not only that, Sam, but you don't even require batteries!"

He said the reason he'd probably never again get laid is that he'd have to wonder just what the hell was wrong with a woman who would want to be with him. Kind of like "what club would I want to belong to that would have me as a member."

"Dan, I think I am going to go and live my dreams."

And I surmised that he was going to take a nap. We parted our ways.

Later that day Sam stopped by my place and we got to talking about our Catholic upbringings. He told me how his family was pretty uptight. It wasn't so much that they preached the Bible. They were just pretty conservative in their views on how he and his siblings should be raised.

I said that I thought my family was pretty much along the same lines, though as I was about to find out that he had me beat more than a little.

"Sam, I remember my mother telling me that my father didn't even like me saying the word 'jeez.' I guess it sounded too much like Jesus, and she told me to stop. My father didn't really say a lot about what he expected, or his feelings, but he didn't have to. He was a man of few words but of a character that I will always try to achieve, even if I really don't see that happenin'."

I had sliced up a few tomatoes and put a slice of mozzarella and some balsamic vinegar on each slice. We were enjoying them when another camper stopped by. Her name was Judy (the campground had more than a few Judys).

She tried one. "Dan, these are fantastic. Now the only thing you need to do to them is add some parsley... just a little."

"Judy, I find that such a typical statement from a woman. First they say how much they love you because you're so great, and the next thing you know, they're telling you what you need to change. If my tomatoes are so good, why change them?" I took the plate away from her. "Go make your own as perfect as you need them to be."

She went on her way and Patty stopped by. Patty had been coming down here for a few years with a friend of hers. (She liked my tomatoes the way they were.)

We told her we had been talking about our parents raising us and Sam continued, "In my family, my mother wouldn't even let us say the word 'panties.' We had to smell them."

Patty and I looked at each other, and I'm sure my mouth had to be hanging open. Neither one of us knew what to say.

All I could come up with was "Excuse me?" I thought maybe I had misunderstood him.

"I said that in my house we were not even allowed to say the word 'panties' and my mother made me smell them."

I thought I was used to Sam's openness and his honesty when we talked. I liked it, but I was really surprised at this, and I was taken more than a little aback this time.

Patty apparently was not quite ready for Sam's candor. She abruptly stood up, not even bothering to look at us. As she turned and walked away, all she said was, "I think this is man's talk, and I really don't believe I want to be any part of it."

Patty hauled her ass out of there. If this had been a cartoon, there would have been a cloud of dust left in her wake. She never looked back as she left us to our "man talk."

Sam looked at me with bewilderment. He had no clue about what had just happened. "Dan, what in the hell was that all about?"

Sam spoke highly of his family. Hell, he spoke highly of everyone. Even though we'd shared a lot of personal stories, this one had caught me off guard.

"Sam, you can't be serious?" He still looked confused, so I continued, "Sam, are you for real? You can't really think that in most people's lives that would be considered okay. The smelling of your sister's panties is really kind of weird."

His expression changed from one of bewilderment to one of absolute shock. His jaw dropped and his eyebrows went up as he jumped up out of his chair. "*WHAT?* Dan, what I said was *SPELL*, not *SMELL*! In my house we were not even allowed to say the word 'panty.' We had to *SPELL* it." He continued his denials. "I SAID *SPELL* IT! NOT *SMELL* IT!"

I burst out laughing and it got to the point I was actually crying, my sides hurting so bad that I had to tell Sam to stop with his explanations. The more he tried to explain, the harder I laughed.

Sam's face was red and all he could say was "I have to find Patty and explain."

I told him to not say anything. "Sam, it's a whole lot more fun this way."

Huntington's was not only robbing Sam of his motor skills, but sometimes even his speech was affected, not so much in his pronunciation of words, but the words he thought he was speaking were not always the same ones he spoke.

"Dan, I can't believe you thought that of me."

"Sam, your secret is safe me and I really doubt that Patty will be repeating that tidbit of information to anyone. Besides that, no one will believe her anyway. However, they just might believe that your mother did catch you sniffing those panties. You know what? I might have to go up to the Liars' Bench tomorrow and see if I can help with this story, to make sure that those who like to gossip get it correct."

Sam hung his head and started to laugh as he continued to proclaim his innocence.

"Sam, I hope you don't have a prior engagement because I've got some fish that are in need of cooking. All right, let's change the subject and get back to what woman would possibly find interesting in you. I have heard talk around this place about a few that find you attractive."

He smiled and asked what I was talking about.

"There's that girl on the point who lost her husband a few years ago. I heard her say just how handsome and nice you were."

He shook his head. "Dan, they took her license away because she's legally blind and eighty years old."

I mentioned Linda from the Electric section and Sam still had his excuses.

"Dan, she tips the scales at 485 pounds."

"Sam, I think that might be the very reason that you will never be laid again. You, sir, are a picky mother fucker!"

The day's light was waning and I brought out my iron skillet pot (a Dutch oven) and I put a little oil in it. Some breaded fish and some sliced potatoes went into that oil. After eating and a little conversation later, Sam went back to his place.

I retired as well. I went to bed content in knowing that my world was nice. I work my ass off not so much to get ahead, though my efforts are rewarded with appreciating and realizing that there are a few precious moments that create memories.

It takes time away from my day-to-day existence to know how good my life and people are. Life is pretty damn good if you get outside of yourself and appreciate what you have and what others share.

Chapter 17

Three Sixes

The next morning as Sam sat down he was still trying to explain what he had meant to say the previous evening. I began to laugh, and the more he explained the harder I laughed.

"Dan, I really can't believe you thought that about me."

Though he was still a little flustered, it wasn't long before Sam joined right in with me laughing just as hard.

"Sam, if you are okay with the things you've done, I think I will be okay with it as well. I try not to judge others' lifestyles."

With Sam, I had become aware of the simple things in life that truly matter, or maybe he just made me less concerned with the day-to-day things that seem important at the time. I think most people trying to get ahead or to maintain do not appreciate the here and now. It's memories that will either leave us rich or broken when we get old.

"Sam, I think I should go up to the Liars' Bench and make sure that any rumor started about you is put into its proper place."

"Let me go, Dan. I need today's paper anyways."

A little while later, Sam returned with a copy of the *Miami Herald* as well as some bacon and eggs.

"Sam, I guess we'll be having scrambled eggs today. Knowing the way you tend to drop things, or shake them up a bit, the eggs will probably be broken."

Seeing the paper, I asked him why he had brought back the *Miami Herald*.

"Dan, it's the weekend, and they only sell *USA Today* on weekdays."

I said I already knew that *USA Today* wasn't even today's news that it was yesterday's. "Now you're telling me that *USA Today* is not only yesterday's news, but if you buy it on Sunday, it'll actually be news from Thursday? Let's not even mention getting it on a Monday when it'll be news from three days ago. Sam, I think you're getting ripped off. How can they get away with calling it *USA Today* when it's the day before at best. I think a better title would be 'The USA of Yesterday's News.'"

Sam knew that a lot of my comments weren't worth commenting on, and I guess this was one of those times. He sat there reading a section of the newspaper and I did the same.

When I came across an article about Asians getting plastic surgery to make their eyes more oval to make them look more "Western," I commented, "Hey Sam, I have an idea for a business. This article claims that some people in the Far East want to look more like we do. I am thinking that perhaps the skin that we lost during our childhood emasculation could be given back! There has to be a market for guys that want their foreskin back. We could use the skin left over from their surgery to help hide our 'heads.' What do you think?"

If nothing else, he seemed amused. "Well, it would give new meaning to the term 'hoodwinked.' What do you want to call this business? Winkie Dinkies? You know what I think? I think that you are not quite right. We import too many things from China already."

I said to Sam that it was pretty sad we no longer seem to export much of anything from this country anymore.

"Dan, we still seem to have a lock on our export of cigarettes to the rest of the world, and unless they come up with a Bok Choy-like tobacco, we have nothing to worry about."

He buried his head back in his paper, and I proceeded to make our breakfast.

He laughed and started talking about an article he was reading. "Dan, there seems to be this leader of his own church who claims he's the Antichrist, right down to having a tattoo of the number 666 on his arm."

I looked up from my pan of frying bacon and immediately turned it off, serving Sam some that was a whole lot short of crispy. It was still dripping its fat onto his plate while I served it to him. In fact, it was barely cooked.

"Dan, this bacon really looks good, but I try to watch my diet and I would rather it be cooked a little more."

"Sam, if what you're telling me is true, you can eat your bacon anyway you want it. You know what? I think I'll even pour us both a cup of the grease to dunk our toast in. Sam, the end of the world is at hand. The Antichrist has arrived, and Armageddon is about to take place. THE APOCALYPSE IS UPON US! Dammit, man, there is no need to worry about tomorrow any longer! Eat your bacon as you wish and drink the lard left behind."

He handed me back his plate and I put the bacon back in the frying pan while he continued reading the paper.

After he had it finished, he said, "Dan, it says that this person used to claim that he was the Son of God, that he was Jesus returning to bring salvation to all those who truly believed, but apparently that turned out not to be too profitable."

I couldn't imagine why people would follow Lucifer himself over the Son of God. "So what you are trying to tell me, Sam, is that it's better to say that you are Satan rather than Jesus?"

He looked at me as if I was nothing more than a naive little child. "Well, hell yes, Dan. Just think about it for a minute."

He gave me a little time to digest. After a minute, I said, "I still don't get it."

"Dan, there is no competition. Just who in the hell is going to claim that they're the spawn of Satan or Lucifer or the very Devil himself? He is even getting free advertising. This article alone takes up half a page."

Sam was in awe of both the genius of this guy and the sadness of his followers, those only looking to be accepted or in need of someone to follow. "Dan, these people don't just tithe; they give as much as fifty percent."

"Sam, why don't you start your own church. We can call it 'The church of Sam.'"

"No, if anything, I'd want to be a Buddhist. At least their ministers don't wear Rolexes."

Sam told about the time he and his wife went to Thailand for six weeks after he closed on a real estate transaction. Apparently he'd made more than a few bucks on the deal.

"Dan, it was such a beautiful country and the people were amazing. We would stay at the best places, and every night the entertainment at the hotel would be female impersonators on stage. They were accepted by everyone in that country. Their belief was that if God created that person that way, then who the hell were they to question God's work? They never judged others who did no one else harm."

And all I could think of was it must be a hell of a place, a country where people accept those that are different and not hurting anyone else. Hell, they actually embraced them and put them on display.

I told Sam that my sister Dee had been to that country on a bike tour and she called it "The land of a thousand smiles." She told me that even when riding through the countryside all the rice farmers would stop their work as they rode by and stand up, smiling and waving.

"That's your sister from Colorado?"

"It most certainly is, and can you believe she went from such a simple name as Hochreiter to a complicated name like Wommeldorf? When she divorced, she kept her last name of Wommeldorf over the Hochreiter name of her forefathers. Can you believe the nerve? Not only that, but she and her friends now refer to her as Sandy as opposed to Dee! Even one better, Sam, she went from a social worker helping troubled kids to a pistol packin' mama working for the state of Colorado as a probation officer!"

"The audacity of some people."

Sam said that in Thailand the people only wanted to do good in this life so they could proceed on to the next and hope to do even better till they were accepted in the afterlife.

He continued reading and came across another article that said the minimum wage was going to be raised. He asked me what I thought about that.

I told him that it might not be a bad thing if everyone had to pay it, though being a small businessman I have to compete against those that pay their employees cash under the table, and it might make it tougher. He thought it was a good thing.

"Why's that, Sam? Are you thinking of getting back into the workforce?"

"No, even if they find a cure for my disease, I don't think I would ever work again. It just isn't that important to me anymore. I no longer have a lot of needs. My life since retiring is pretty simple and I really enjoy it. In fact, I think it's perfect."

I asked him what his plans were for the day. He said that he wanted to visit with a few people from around the campground. They were calling for rain so I would be land bound as well.

He headed to parts unknown and I headed to the showers.

Later that day, I was walking by Sam's when he waved me over. He was talking on the phone and all I heard was his end of the conversation.

"You're having your mother for dinner?" There was a pause and he said, "Well I wonder how she's going to taste?"

I sat down and it began to rain. We got under Sam's canopy and it soon began to pour. I looked at him and asked if he played pool. There was a pool table and other games upfront at the Community Center. They even had a TV for those of us without.

Sam said that he did play pool, although he sucked, and it was agreed that when there was a lull in the rain we'd head upfront.

He normally rode his bicycle around camp, though lately he had taken to walking at least when I was with him, probably because I didn't have a bike. He said that he was always in pain, and it was the only time he mentioned it. His legs always hurt.

I told him to ride his bike, that I'd meet him up there.

"No, Dan, I'd rather walk beside you than ride alone."

"Thanks, Sam, though I'm not too sure how to take that."

When we walked, he had gotten into the habit of putting his hand on my shoulder and plugging forward. I didn't know whether it helped steady him or he just wanted to make sure I didn't get away.

While walking, I looked at him. "Sam, I'll race you to the front."

He looked over at me and told me that not only was he up for that, but he would have no problem in beating me. "How much is the bet, Dan?"

"Sam, I know what a cheap bastard you are, and I don't want to bet more than I think you'll pay. How does a nickel sound?"

I touched my toes, then touched my nose and reached for the stars, making sure I was limbered up and ready for the race. I ran in place for a second or two and said to him, "Dammit, I'm outta shape, but I think I can still take you."

Sam laughed, latched on to my shirt and let out a holler for all to hear, "LET THE GAMES BEGIN!"

I told him that the only reason he was holding on to my shirt was so that I couldn't run ahead.

"I realize that, Dan, and I really am sorry, but you have to realize that I am working with a bit of a handicap here."

We continued on our walk upfront, all the while Sam holding on to my shirt and just a half step behind me. He suddenly stopped and gave me a jerk back as he stepped forward and in front of me proclaiming, "Dan, I just won the race. That was officially where the back of the campground ended and the front began."

I protested that we weren't yet to the front.

"That was the finish line! I've been coming here a lot longer than you, and that was the dividing line we just crossed from the back to the front." He held out his hand and yelled, "NOW WHERE'S MY NICKEL?"

No wonder Sam had done so well in the corporate world.

We got to the pool table and I headed over to the office for some quarters that the table required to play. Upon returning, I mentioned to Sam that I would be shooting left-handed to help compensate him for his lack of dexterity.

And of course Sam had to come up with a comment. "I suppose you're left-handed?"

"Bite me, Sam. I'm trying to level the playing field here. I have never been all about winning. I just like a close, fun game."

I wasn't worth a crap left-handed, and within a relatively short period of time Sam had three balls dropped in to my zero.

He looked at me, trying to sound sympathetic. "Dan, are you sure you don't want to shoot right-handed?"

"I am sure, Sam. I am merely building up your confidence so it'll be that much more sweet when I send you crashing back down to the earth after building up your ego to the point that I seem just another casualty that you have left behind. And, Sam, *you* are going *down*! Hey, now that I've increased your portfolio with that nickel, are we betting?"

"Of course we're betting, I figure a dollar a ball sounds good."

Of course he figured that was good. He was already three balls ahead. The next two shots of Sam's were a little bit off the mark and he put two of my balls in, then I made it even (I thought) by sinking one of my own.

Three balls each.

Sam had striped balls and mine were solid, and before too awfully long we were both trying for the eight ball and the win. After way too many attempts, I finally sank it and told Sam that he owed me a dollar.

Sam looked at me straight-faced and said, "No, Dan. We were playing for a dollar a ball, and I put two of yours in, so you owe me for them as well. Actually, you now owe me a dollar plus a nickel for the race."

I gave him his dollar and he looked at me. "WHERE'S MY NICKEL?"

I looked back at him. "Sam, you ain't nothing but a two-bit hustler, and yes I owe you a nickel."

Sam explained to me one dollar and a nickel was a whole lot more than two bits and that if I wanted to redeem myself, we could play a couple of games of ping-pong. I went back to the store and got the paddles and a ping-pong ball. I never mentioned playing for any money. Sam's mind would figure out a way to compensate for his lack of physical prowess.

I started out playing left-handed and couldn't even hit the ball, so I went to my right hand and we decided that we would just try to keep the ball in play. It didn't matter if it went off the ceiling or wall. We kept it going back and forth, somewhat. We weren't about to represent our country in the Olympics, but we did have fun. We actually kept it in play sometimes.

The rain had let up and Sam went about his meanderings within the camp, as did I. I told him I was cooking an Italian dish later that day, greens and beans, and that he was invited.

"Well, hell yes I'll be there! I love the thought of Italian food cooked by a German-American camping in the Florida Keys without a stove."

I told him that I did indeed have a stove even if it was an outdoor camping type.

Later that day he came by. I was cooking escarole and beans and had some Italian sausage on the grill. He was all but drooling. He couldn't even wait till my concoction was through cooking. "Dan, that sausage looks done."

"It is. I am only waiting for the rest of the food to be done so I can mix it in."

Sam was enjoying the smell of the sausage as it permeated the air around us, and I was trying his patience. I could tell the sausage was weighing on his mind. He was Italian after all, and the smell of it grilling was leaving him more than a little hungry.

"Smell that sausage, Sam?"

"Yes I do, and it smells wonderful'"

I put the cover on the grill and turned off the vents and just sat there with Sam.

After more than a few comments, Sam looked at me and said, "I think they say it's absence that makes the heart grow fonder, not anticipation."

I laughed and finally offered him a sausage even before the rest of the meal was prepared.

He all but devoured my offering, proclaiming his thanks and what a wonderful cook I was.

I told him that I put the "oo" in food and the "eff" in chef. He didn't argue.

Once the meal was prepared (properly) with the sausage cut up and mixed in with the rest, I served Sam a bowl along with some Cuban bread.

"Sorry about the bread, Sam. It ain't no Italian like up North, but it's the best I could find in Florida."

A few beers later we parted our ways. It had been a fun day.

Chapter 18

Montgomery Ward

The next morning Sam arrived and I poured him a cup of coffee, and upon taking his first sip he immediately spit it out. "Dammit, that's really hot!"

"Sorry, Sam, I gave you the first cup. I hadn't even tasted it nor tested its temperature for you. If nothing else you now have an inkling of what I go through every morning for you."

"Dan, if you were McDonald's, I'd be calling my lawyer to see if I had a case. I think I'd probably sue you."

"Again, Sam, let me say how truly sorry I am. I'm sure if you drive down the road a bit you'll find a billboard with a lawyer on it that'll take your case, or you could go up to the Electric section and find a television and wait ten minutes or so and have the names of a few more that'll take your case. You know what I think?"

"No, Dan, though I do believe you're about to tell me."

"Sam, if it weren't for lawyers, we wouldn't even need any lawyers."

Sam let out a laugh.

"Lawyers go against other lawyers, and they appear before a judge, usually another lawyer, and the clients pay. As far as my coffee is concerned, you get what you pay for." I offered him a refund.

He declined and said that the suffering was worth the price of admission to my world. He wanted to know how my writing was going.

"Slowly."

He asked if he'd ever told me about an article he had written about hunting dogs.

"No way, Sam! You actually have a story written? I suppose it wasn't worthy of being published."

He told me that it had been published and he had a copy someplace and would try to find it. I didn't bother telling him that he'd mentioned it before.

"Sam, I recently wanted to get my mom a dog and I saw a commercial on TV about saving abused animals. I got on their website, hoping to find a local place where I could adopt a rescue dog for her. They showed pictures of neglected, abused animals. They wanted nineteen dollars a month, every month, to help abused dogs, *and* there was a famous singer asking for my money. Sam, they only wanted money, and I only wanted a dog. I called their number and they asked for dollars to feed the dogs and there I was trying to find a dog to feed."

"Dan, when I was in Catholic school, the nuns wanted us to sell dolls for five dollars each. They said that every doll that we sold would feed a pagan in Africa for their entire life."

"Sam, how could five dollars feed someone for life?"

"Dan, that's the same question a friend asked the nun and she said, 'They're pygmies. They don't eat that much.'"

I asked Sam if he would be exercising that day.

"Dan, the last time I was there, I was on an exercise bicycle and someone had farted and it smelled terrible. I thought, my God, how embarrassing. When I got off the bike, I realized that I had shit myself. I cleaned up the best I could, but it was still not a nice ride back for the people I rode with. I'm not sure I'll ever go again"

I told him that if it happened again and anyone asked if he had just farted, he should reply, "No, I pooped too."

Sam had brought over some bacon and some eggs. We cooked them up and talked for a while.

"Sam, my nephew Jake is coming in for a day or two. If you ain't got any plans for today, then stop on by. He's an ex-Navy man. You might find him someone that you have something in common with for a change. He recently got out of the military after completing his obligation and he is about to go over to Kuwait for a year, working for a military contractor. He thought he'd come down to visit before leaving."

Jake's father was my sister's husband, who passed away in his early thirties when Jake was just a child. His father had broken an ankle, and while it was healing, a blood clot found his heart. Jake was now at that age where he was trying to figure out what he wanted in life and was taking a little time to have some fun before heading overseas.

Later on that day, my nephew arrived. We sat around and I told him some stories about his dad, who had been not only my brother-in-law but a very close friend. I doubted Jake had too many memories of his own.

I told him of the times his father (Jim) and I would go fishing and would wind up hitting about every bar on the way home and of the dumb things we did and the laughs we had. I told him of the love and devotion his father had for his family after he and his sister came along.

Later, Sam stopped by. We all had a few beers. Sam asked Jake where all he'd been to in the Navy. Every place Jake mentioned Sam either knew a lot about or had been there himself.

Anyone Sam met he would know something of the place they were from, whether it be what their economy was based on or what sights it was known for. It was fun listening to him talk with others.

I spoke up, "Sam, you'll like this one. My nephew's name was almost Montgomery Ward. If his Dad had had his way, it *would* have been Montgomery Ward."

Sam and Jake looked at each other then back at me.

"What do you mean?" Jake asked.

"Jake, no one ever told you before? Well, now that I think of it, why would they?"

I told him that Montgomery Ward was the name of a company that made washers and dryers, as well as other appliances. "You see, Jake, your mom and dad went on a vacation to Florida and stayed with your Uncle Philip. Well, they were in the house alone and your mother was doing laundry when your dad got that urge and picked her up and placed her on that washer from Montgomery Ward and, lo and behold, you were conceived that day. Your dad thought 'Montgomery Ward' would have been an appropriate name."

I looked at Jake and told him that when I saw his sister Katie, I'd have to tell her what her name almost was.

I didn't say anything else.

Jake looked at me and raised his eyebrows. "Well, Uncle Dan? You can't stop there. What did my dad want to name *Katie*?"

"Aw, Jake, I probably shouldn't have said anything. It was something said between me and your dad, after all."

"Uncle Dan, you told me what my name almost was. The least you can do is tell me what sister's almost was!"

"Okay, but just remember, you asked."

"Your father wanted to name your sister Sara Lee."

He looked at me, a little confused. "Sara Lee? Don't they make cakes or desserts or something?"

"They made frosting as well. You see, Jake, one day your mom was making a cake and there was a bowl of that frosting on the table. Your dad took some and put a little on your mom, then she put a little on him, and I guess they both had a sweet tooth, and before you knew it, Sara Lee was being conceived."

"Uncle Dan!"

I had a few steaks on hand, which I grilled along with some potatoes and heated up some canned vegetables. We continued talking into the evening.

Sam headed back to his camper. Jake and I talked a while longer and had a few more beers till we called it a night.

Chapter 19

Go West Young Man

The following morning I was up and outside with my pot of coffee on the stove when Sam arrived. Jake was still in bed. "The youth of today apparently need more sleep than we do," I said to Sam. (Jake was in his early twenties.)

Sam defended him, saying that he had just driven down here and was probably still a little weary from the road.

Jake popped his head out of the camper and sat down next to us. He showed us that the young'uns had no problem hanging with us old farts.

"I have been awake and was just waiting for someone to make some coffee," he said.

I looked at Sam. "See! They don't even know how to boil water!"

I told Sam that Jake and I would be heading to Key West to do the tourist thing, if he wanted to come along.

He declined. He said it was too hard on his legs, but I suspect that he thought it would be good for me to spend some time bonding with my nephew.

We sat around for a while, drinking our coffee and talking about nothing in particular. I got up and went inside my camper and brought out some corned beef hash, never bothering to ask anyone if they were hungry.

I put some water on the stove, and while bringing it to a boil, I toasted some bread over the other burner. I dropped some eggs into the boiling water to poach them while heating up the corned beef hash. It was a nice way to get the day started: family and friends, coffee and food.

After a pot or two or three of coffee, Sam left and I headed to the showers. Upon my return Jake did the same.

I went back to Sam's to ask one last time if he wanted to go, and he again declined.

Jake and I headed to Key West for a day of debauchery.

Key West is as far South as you can go in the continental United States. Cuba is only ninety miles away. It's the tropics, and it's always warm (at least by most of the country's standards).

From striving artists living their dream to millionaires showing their wealth, from gays and straights to derelicts and those claiming to be trying to save them, (from what, I don't know), it's a place where people enjoy, or at least tolerate, everything different. I think that most people here don't just tolerate, they enjoy all the weirdos, and the police let people enjoy as long as they are not out of line.

I took Jake to a bar/restaurant. We both had some conch chowder. I had a beer and Jake a few Margaritas, and we both had their special of seared tuna. It was getting to be late afternoon and we headed to Mallory Square on the westernmost part of the island to watch the celebration of the sunset. We stopped at a bar and got a couple of drinks to go—there are no open container laws here.

People gather along the break wall to watch the sun as it goes over the horizon, and street performers entertain the crowd for tips. It's fun, and something as beautiful as a sunset is something most of us don't take the time to enjoy unless away from our regular life.

We hit a few more bars and ended up at the local topless joint. It was the least I could do for him. For a while he would be in a country that allowed neither nude women nor booze. It was all only for him. I personally would never consider partaking of such endeavors.

We managed to find our way back to camp and wasted no time in having a few more cocktails till we both decided it was time for some sleep.

Chapter 20

Just Another Day in Paradise

The next morning I awoke and the sun was already up. In fact, it was already well past having risen. I had no idea of the time, though the time of day didn't really matter. I was on vacation. I made some coffee and Jake and I sat around waiting for a little caffeine to help us get over the previous day's and night's festivities.

Sam hadn't come around, so I went by his trailer to see what was going on. He was sitting outside at his table and said he'd stopped by earlier, but no one seemed to be awake yet. He thought that I had probably stayed up kind of late.

"Well thanks, Sam. I guess you are more considerate of my feelings than I was giving you credit for."

Sam also said that he knew if he woke me, the coffee would probably be crap, and I would have been grumpy, and that would hardly be a nice way to start such a beautiful day. "Other than the coffee, I guess it's like most mornings, Dan, but I keep hoping that my company will rub off on you and make you a little bit better of a person."

I told him the coffee was done now and tasting pretty damn good and if he wanted a cup, it was ready, and he had better act a little more like he appreciated it.

He followed me back to my place and helped me and Jake turn those coffee grounds into the start of a new day, or maybe a better afternoon.

Sam said it was almost nine o'clock and the day had long ago started without me.

"Sam, it's not the first day, nor do I think it will be my last, that will start without me while I am here."

We sat around talking for a little while till that pot of coffee and another was finished and we went about our day.

Jake and I went into town for some bait for the fish that we hoped we'd be taking for a boat ride back to camp and the grill. We picked up some fried chicken from the local Deon's convenience store for our lunch and headed out for a day of fun in the sun. Fishing and family go well together.

We caught some mangrove snapper and a few grunts, a few porgies, though no Bess. Back on shore, I cleaned the fish and Jake and I ate and exchanged some stories. Later on, Sam stopped by and we had a couple of cocktails.

Jake spoke of his time in the Navy while he was stationed in the Far East in Okinawa and his time exploring the Philippines and Thailand. His upcoming time he'd be spending in Kuwait working on computers for a military contractor. Sam wanted to know all about it.

I was more than a little tired after the previous night out on the town and went to bed, leaving Jake and Sam to talk of life in the Far East.

The next morning I awoke and started perking some coffee. It finished brewing, but Jake and Sam were still not with me. I assumed that the night before they had talked about me and neither one of them was ready for another day of my nonsense, but I didn't care. (Actually the sun was just barely up and they had stayed up till whenever.)

It was Jake's last day, or rather morning, and he was young. I wasn't the least bit bothered by waking him, so I said, "Get your ass up!" as I set a cup of coffee beside him.

I didn't mind going over to Sam's place either to tell him to get up. I enjoyed his company and my days here were limited. He once told me that he was a selfish man, and I supposed I might be too.

"Sam! Arise and get your lazy ass out of bed!"

He stuck his head out the door and I handed him a cup of coffee. "Good morning to you as well, Dan."

I went back to my place. Jake was sitting there with his coffee. I sat across from him, and not long after Sam made his way over as well.

The two of them kind of sat there, and all I could do was smile as I almost yelled out, "And a top o' the morning to ya, me laddies!"

They looked at each other, shaking their heads. When they looked at me, what else could I do but smile? Family and friends are a good combination.

We sat there for a while before I heated up the frying pan and a little butter. I had some onions and red peppers and threw them in till they began to soften. A bunch of eggs scrambled added to the mix and all was well.

After a while, Sam told us that he needed a little more beauty sleep and headed back to his place. Jake and I exchanged our hugs and he went off into manhood.

Later, Sam came back and wanted to know how much I knew about cell phones. I told him that I knew quite a lot.

"You see, Sam, in order to start a conversation, you push some buttons that represent who you want to call, and then press another button. To start a conversation, you press SEND, and to end the conversation you press END."

"Dan, my battery doesn't hold a charge. I bought a new battery and that doesn't seem any better. At least they told me it was a new battery. After I left and thought about it, I realized the battery they'd given me was taken out of a drawer and already unwrapped. That's one thing about having this disease. I don't always catch things like that."

I said to Sam that we could go back to that store and exchange it, and he said that he didn't know if it was used or not. He was upset with himself for not having paid closer attention. I was going to the flea market later that day and told him that one of the booths had cell phone accessories, and if he wanted to go along I was sure we'd find him his battery. He said he would like that, but he would only accept a ride if we could go to a place he knew of that had a "happy hour" and two-for-one specials and that he would be buying.

"Sam, we'll discuss who pays later."

And he headed off to get himself ready.

I drove around to pick him up and he said he wasn't really comfortable buying a battery from a vendor at a flea market after suspecting a store hadn't even done him right. It was decided we'd go to a store in Marathon that represented his cell phone provider.

Sam was a little agitated and moving about more so than usual. "Dan, one of the things about this disease is once you get something in your mind, you latch onto it and dwell on it. If it weren't for Huntington's, I know this shouldn't be such a big deal. Every person I know is in that phone, and I don't have their numbers anyplace else. Some people like my sister have as many as five numbers: her business line, her cell phone, her business cell, her home phone, and her fax line. If I lose this phone, I'm fucked."

All my encouragement of saying we'd find a way to save his phone and those numbers was only met with his concerns. I suppose that was one of the reasons he had been so successful. He would cover his ass every which way to make sure that he didn't overlook any detail. Huntington's was slowly taking that ability away, and he was well aware of that.

We went to the store and upon arriving, we were ignored while the employees spoke among themselves and answered the phone. There were no other customers. After a few minutes, or maybe five, I looked on the counter. A blank invoice had the store's number on it, so I called. One of the people who had been standing there answered and I explained Sam's dilemma and was told to come right in, that it should not be too big of a problem.

When I asked him about a wait, he said there shouldn't be one. I said, "Good, then hang up the phone and wait on us. I'm the guy standing in front of you that's been waiting for someone to acknowledge us."

He just looked up and said that he really didn't like wiseasses and told someone else to take care of us.

Sam looked at me and said, "Thanks, Dan, though I really don't think you helped matters all that much."

Sam explained to the kid that came to help us the problem of the phone not holding a charge. After some testing, he was told that his phone was in need of replacement. Sam agreed to a new contract and a new phone along with the promise that all his old numbers would be in his new phone. In the process of doing this, all of his numbers were erased from his old phone and duplicated into his new, leaving Sam at a loss as to how to identify one number from the next. The numbers were there though not the names associated with them, and all numbers were duplicated.

I wasn't really sure just what had happened, but I knew that Sam had to keep his life in order so he could to some degree keep in control. I knew this wasn't a good thing. They started talking in technical terms that were more than a little over my head. The counter kid went over to a woman and explained just what he'd done. Her questions to him were explicit, and his answers were as well.

The whole while Sam was listening, his body movements, or rather his lack of control over them, became more pronounced. This was not good in the world of a person who was losing control without someone else's screw-ups adding to it. Sam was not happy.

This woman came over and explained to Sam that what was in his old phone were not in his memory card and that his new phone could only correctly copy a memory card. It sounded like a whole bunch of malarkey to me. I think the counter kid had messed up and all Sam said to no one in particular, "I'm screwed."

I believe the woman was the wife to the guy I'd spoken to on the phone and they both owned this place. He came over and asked the counter kid just what Sam had paid for and then turned to Sam and offered him some software at no charge that would fix the problem.

I looked over at Sam and he said to this guy, "You screwed it up! You fix it!"

It was a side of Sam I hadn't seen, and this showed me again of why he had been successful. He would accept nothing less than what had been agreed upon.

To the store's credit, or to the woman's, she spent the next two hours going through Sam's phone and deleting all duplicates, then getting the names from his old phone to correspond with the new phones numbers that had been transferred.

Sam took his new phone and sat down in the store, reviewing all its features that he required so he totally understood before leaving. He asked a few questions and got answers he was comfortable with. Anything he was unsure of, he went to this woman and she would explain.

Satisfied with both his phone and knowledge of it, he looked up at me and said, "I think I'm okay, Dan. Give me a call on my phone." I did and Sam answered, "Okay, Dan, now I am going to call you." He did and I answered.

Sam was comfortable with his new phone. He knew his limitations and had to make sure that he made things as simple as possible.

I have had the pleasure of meeting many a person in my life, but Sam was special insofar as his perspective on his life, his known demise, and his dealing with all the obstacles. No one I've ever met came close to this guy.

We left the store around five o'clock or so and Sam let out a yell. "It's Happy Hour, Dan!" The restaurants would have their specials going on, and he was ready not only to eat but to have a cocktail or two.

Just down the road there was a Tiki bar he had been to before and wanted to try again.

We arrived and were told to "just pick a seat anywhere." We took a small table that allowed a view of the ocean to the west. It would allow us to see the sun as it set over the ocean.

We ordered a Margarita and a dozen oysters. It being happy hour, our order was doubled and we both received one of each. It was wonderful. We ordered a tuna steak lightly seared and another Margarita as well as another dozen oysters.

Sam said he thought I might have screwed up when I had called on the phone to get service.

"What can I tell ya, Sam? That is Wegmans' fault (a local grocery store in Rochester). They demand that their employees take care of their customers, and I just don't understand why any employer would expect less.

"The other day I went to a store in Marathon and had a bunch of stuff in my basket and couldn't find any propane bottles. Sam, I looked around and couldn't find them and asked three different employees where they were and got the same 'Well I think they might be over in...'

"The last person was at the customer service counter and she said the same thing, 'Well, I think that maybe...' Three different people and none of them knew or would find out. I asked her if anyone that worked here knew anything and set my basket on the counter and said, 'I think maybe you can figure out where you can put these items,' and walked out.

We watched the sun set over the ocean and Sam was again in limited control of his world. I let him have his way with me. (I didn't even try to get the bill).

It had been a nice day. We headed back to our campers. I did not attempt any newfound writings.

Chapter 21

The "Cock" Republic

Another "royal" day arrived along with Sam. I stood up and bowed before him. "Your assholiness, both your coffee and me, your humble servant, have not only been anticipating but oh so looking forward to, your arrival."

I poured him a cup of coffee.

Sam grumbled that he wasn't quite sure why he put up with my crap.

"The reason you put up with me, Sam, is that I have the best coffee between here and the Atlantic Ocean, maybe even beyond."

"Dan, you have the *only* coffee between here and the Atlantic Ocean. The only thing between this site and the ocean is a whole bunch of mangrove trees, some animals, and maybe a homeless person who managed to get away without the law noticing his presence for a night."

I told him that I still had bragging rights and not to be so trivial with the reason why.

"In fact, Dan, the ocean being to the east, I guess you *might* have the best coffee between here and Africa."

"Now you understand, Sam."

"Dan, this really is good coffee and I thank you for it." We sat down and Sam looked at me. "Dan, let's go to Key West today."

I was more than a little surprised. I'd been asking him for quite a while if he'd like to go do the "tourist thing," but he always declined. His medicine left him too tired, and he'd said once that he was in constant pain and walking added to it.

For whatever reason, he had decided that he felt up to it and would indeed like to go. I was only too happy to accommodate him.

I told him that if I had to put up with his miserable ass for the day, the least he could do would be to let me buy breakfast. I got up and started chopping up a few potatoes, some onions, peppers, and tomatoes.

Sam asked what I was doing.

"Sam, everything I am about to cook I bought, and I'm not about to let it go to waste so you can ogle a pretty waitress and cost me another twenty bucks."

I told him to stop his bellyaching. If we were going to do the Key West thing, it was going to be for the whole day, not just a couple of hours, and he had better get his beauty rest in before we left.

I fried up the whole concoction of stuff in some olive oil and added a couple of fried eggs that had been cooked in butter, and threw it on top. Sam never said a word. I guess he had learned not to talk with his mouth full.

Shortly after that, he headed back to his place to rest for a little while. And I took care of my morning's rituals.

A few hours later, Sam stopped by and said, "Dan, I am ready. Let's go to Key West." Sam loaded his ass into my truck and we headed down the road.

We were driving along over the bridges, passing through the various towns, when Sam blurted out at the top of his lungs, "FUCK!"

I looked over at him. "Sam, just what in the hell was that all about?"

"Sorry, Dan, I was just thinking about when I was in college at Michigan State. A bunch of us would go to the stadium to see our football team play and there was always this one guy in the parking lot before the game that would play the trumpet. He would blow away and he was really quite good at it. Then suddenly, for no apparent reason, he'd stop in the middle of a song, and at the top of his lungs he would scream out every obscenity you could possibly imagine."

Sam learned later that this person had Tourette's syndrome.

"Dan, if I had my choice of any disease, I think I'd like to have Tourette's. Just think about it. You could say anything at any time in any place and you would have a doctor's note saying it was okay—any time, any place. You could be in a hospital, a library, a church, and no one could do anything about it."

"Sam, the church might be the best. Parishioners would cover their children's ears and make the sign of the cross every time you went on a tirade. Not only that, but they would probably say a prayer for you: *Lord above, please help this man for he does not sin by his own volition. It is the Devil upon his tongue. We know him and his heart is pure.*

"I bet with all the doctors you see that one of them would write a letter stating that 'due to your condition you have been known to suffer from a lapse of vocabulary.' And it would be true, Sam. You could walk into the classiest restaurant in town and cuss away."

(Tourette's syndrome is a disease that leaves a person with the inability to control outbursts. Various "tics" sometimes portray themselves in cuss words. The person afflicted has no control. It really is a medical condition... No kidding. I ain't a shittin'.)

We continued driving along and Sam kept up with his nonstop talking. "Dan, did you know that the word 'fuck' is the only word in the English language that to and of itself can form a complete sentence."

"Sam, I'm afraid to ask, though I suppose I have to. Just what in the FUCK are you talking about?"

Sam said that the *only* word in the English language in its various forms that could form a complete sentence without any other words was the word "fuck."

"Let me give you an example, Dan: Fucking fuckers fuck. You see? One word in different forms. In fact, there was actually a course at Michigan State I took that was called 'Fuckisms.'"

"Sam, I do believe that you, sir, are full of poop."

He looked at me with an expression of shock.

"Dan, you have hurt my feelings. I can't believe that you would doubt my word. Me an ex-military man! I am a graduate from Michigan State University. I have survived the discipline of a Catholic education and made it through the corporate world, and you have the audacity to doubt my word?"

I looked at Sam and shook my head. "Well, Mr. Catalano, if there was any doubt before, there isn't now. I know that you graduated with at least a BS degree. I can only hope that my BS can keep up."

He didn't miss a beat. "Anyway, this course was designed to teach us about words, in particular how that one word could be used to form a complete sentence. It was a course taught by the English department I do believe."

"All I can say, Sam, is that if I hurt your feelings by saying you're full of shit, then you'd better get used to it, because I'm sure it won't be the last, and I'm sure I wasn't the first."

Sam told me to give it a try and I gave it my best. "Fuckers fuck."

"There you go, Dan. That was wonderful. One word in different variations, yet a complete sentence. I think my teachers would have been proud of you for that first effort."

I looked at Sam and laughed, and so we began to outdo each other. "Fuck, fuckers fuckingly fucking."

"Fuck fucking fuckers fuckily fucking."

Sam told me that, even without a "higher education," he felt that I would have done quite well in this class.

"All right, Sam, let's see if you can outdo this: Fucking fuckers fuckily fucking, FUCKER!"

Sam was impressed, yet told me that, that last "*fucker*" should probably have been in another sentence.

We both laughed like a couple of adolescents. By the time we were through, I think we had used as many as seven variations in one sentence.

Sam congratulated me. "Dan, I think you might even have done okay in college."

I responded with, "Irregardlessly of my lack of a formal edication, I still gots a bit of common sense."

We were acting like kids. It was foolish; it made absolutely no sense.

It was wonderful.

It was mankind at his finest, and I thought that if Charles Darwin could see us now, he could only hope that the rest of the animal kingdom had fared better. I don't think he'd have thought much of the evolution of my or Sam's ancestors.

We arrived in Key West and I found a parking lot right in the heart of Duval Street where everything and everyone that you wanted to see was and were, maybe even some things and people that you wished you hadn't.

Sam and I headed to the nearest bar and we both ordered a drink. I got a beer and Sam, a Margarita.

What is really wonderful about Key West is that it's a community of the locals that cater to the tourists who come down. The local working people are those living their dream of being in paradise, for the most part eking out a living, yet still living their dream: writers hoping to find Hemingway's inspiration; artists hoping to find their own. It's a community of harmless misfits that accept everyone and their idiosyncrasies of living a life that is fun.

Sam and I finished our drinks and were just taking in the sites when he said he had to pee. Upon his return from the restroom I said that I wanted to take the "Conch Train" tour.

The Conch train is an engine with a conductor (tour guide) that tows a half dozen "cars" around the streets of the city, showing some of its sights and explaining its history.

"Sam, it will be a way to get around the historical part of Key West without walking, and I think it might be interesting to get a little of the background on this place."

Sam liked the idea and told me that the only way he would go is if he could buy the tickets. He didn't appreciate it when I showed him that I had already bought them while he was off taking care of business. I said if he didn't go along on the ride, he would have to wait till I got back, and I would tell the drunk sitting on the sidewalk that I would give him that ticket when I got back if he would keep Sam company till then.

Sam pissed and moaned for a little bit but had a smile on his face as we boarded the train.

It was actually fun, a brief version of the history and a few dumb jokes by the conductor. The tour guide told stories about the town and said, "I can honestly say that I have never had an unhappy day in my life."

Of course I had to chime in with, "I guess you've never been married." That got a few laughs.

Later in the tour he explained that at one time Key West tried to secede from the United States of America to become a nation of its own, and they referred to their newfound country as the "Conch Republic."

Sam yelled out, "No wonder there are so many gays down here. They misunderstood the word 'conch' and thought they had their own nation." (The "ch" in "conch" is pronounced "k.")

The tour ended, and Sam and I headed toward Mallory Square where people gathered to watch and celebrate the sunset and to be entertained by the local street performers. It wasn't quite time for the sun to set so we stopped at a restaurant.

We ordered a drink and some food, and when the waitress appeared with the bill, I didn't even attempt to intercept it (I hoped it was a lot).

A few Margaritas and some food in us, as well as a drink to go, we left and took in the entertainment.

It's a fun show that those who make a living doing "street art" put forth. If you allow yourself, you actually become a part of it. They are part carnival hawkers, acrobats, jugglers, tight rope walkers, and even a cat or two as part of the acts. Some would call upon people in the audience to help them in their acts. Their whole livelihood depends on a few tips from those they entertain. Both Sam and I were entertained and added more than a few bucks to the hat passed around afterwards.

It's amazing how many people are willing to pay five dollars for a drink that'll last a few minutes yet will sneak away without giving so much as a dollar after being entertained by someone trying to make a living.

The sun set and Sam and I headed back to the campground where we hung out for a while, drinking a few rums and talking a whole lot about nothing.

It had been a wonderful day. I was left in awe of a man that enjoyed both his life and all those he came into contact with, and I felt myself fortunate to be among those who were a part of that.

Chapter 22

A Straight Georgian Heard
a Desolate Sound

The next morning came as did Sam. Drinking our first cup of coffee, I told Sam that I hadn't seen a sunrise over the ocean yet this year.

He grabbed his coffee cup and simply said, "Well, then let's go," as he stood up.

We topped off our cups and headed the few hundred yards to the shore, which faced east and the rising of the sun.

Sam put his hand on my shoulder as we walked along to a section of the campground that would give us a view of the sunrise still a little ways off, though the dawn of a new day was enough to light our way.

Every morning for many a year Sam was awake before the sun had risen while camping in the Keys. His site had been on the ocean and the morning's sunrise was one of the gifts he received. Each sunrise never seemed to be quite the same as that of the days before.

Many people comment on the beauty of the sun's rising or it's setting, though it's the clouds or other things along the horizon that makes it different every day. Even smog or dust in the air changes her beauty, often enhancing it and making it special.

I would have to say that we'd picked a good day, but I can't imagine there ever being a bad day to watch the sun rising over the ocean. A dark, narrow bank of clouds on the horizon didn't allow the actual sunrise to be seen as it crested the sea. It reflected those beams of light onto little bands of clouds running parallel over the ocean and scattered upward and outward. The sun's reflection off those ribbons of clouds was absolutely beautiful.

There were reds, oranges, yellows, pinks, and the grays of clouds changing their color as the sun rose. Every ribbon of every cloud seemed to show other colors, as did the sky in between. It was probably a first for both of us because neither one of us spoke.

Back at camp I poured us both another cup of coffee and we were sitting there lost within our own thoughts when Sam asked if I'd ever heard of the "Georgian Straits" or "Desolation Sound."

"No, I have not, Mr. Catalano, though I'm thinkin' that maybe it won't be too awfully long before you'll regale me with one of your many adventures. Please, Samuel, do tell."

And do tell he did. What was so great about our relationship is neither one of us had any other place to be, no calls that had to be answered that wouldn't or couldn't wait, no one to wonder, "Where the hell are you and what are you doing?" I think it's unusual in most people's lives as we grow older, at least in mine it was.

Sam told me that when he was living in Seattle, he came across a boat that was priced to sell. "Dan, it was twenty-eight feet long and had a berth of ten feet. It really wasn't a practical boat for most people. Being ten feet wide you needed special permits to tow it down the road. Every time you wanted to move it anyplace other than on the water, a special permit was required, and that would have been a pain in the ass. For me it was perfect. I kept it in the water at a marina, and anytime I wanted to get away, it was ready."

Sam and I had spoken a lot of our pasts, and I already knew that he had not done too bad with Coldwell Realty. (Actually, I believe he had done pretty damn good.)

He spoke of how that boat took him to places that there were few other ways to get to, except by air or on foot. It was a rugged coastline not easily accessible even by land. There were no roads that allowed access to those shores.

"Dan, I kept my boat at a marina and all I had to do was make a call and they made sure my boat was fueled and ready to go. I'd head north past the Canadian border and into Desolation Sound and The Georgian Straits.

"I had the right boat, Dan, and it wasn't that bad. The tides, currents, and winds would make waves not only big but close together and would beat the crap out of lesser boats."

And I assumed lesser boaters as well.

He would head north into the wilderness with not much more than some cans of Dinty Moore stew and a few other basics: fishing gear, traps, a few cans of vegetables, and a big supply of balls.

"Dan, it was wonderful. I had a marine radio that would allow me to keep in contact with not only my office (through a few intermediaries) but the Coast Guard and an air transport company that acted like a taxi service for people in these wilderness areas."

He said that the air transport was relatively cheap, and though they might not run a tight schedule, they were always there. A call to them would result in a pickup within a few days.

"If I had to get back to the office, they'd pick me up, and they'd return me when I was ready. The boat stayed there tied up till I got back and it was never disturbed. There was no one around to bother it. I'd go for days, if not weeks, without ever seeing anyone."

Sam and I had gotten to the point that we spoke freely of our pasts. From watching him with others, I saw him listening to the stories of others, but I thought maybe he wanted to talk for a change, and with me he found someone willing to listen.

"Dan, I'd set traps in water that was four hundred feet deep and catch tiger prawn."

I looked at him and shook my head. The only time I'd heard of the word "prawn" was in an Australian restaurant selling "shrimp on the barbie."

"Sam, aren't tiger prawn nothing more than a fancy name for big shrimp?"

Sam said that he supposed that was as good a description as any.

"Then why don't you call them what they are? Big shrimp!"

Sam smiled at me and I knew that he was humoring me, as was I him. We both had an understanding of people and knew what buttons to push and how hard, and with me and Sam there were a whole lot of buttons that we both pushed as hard as we wanted.

Sam told of the oysters just lying about for the taking, however many you wanted and whenever they were desired. The water was clean and every shore or shallow water had an abundance.

"Dan, one time I thought I was 'Cool Hand Luke.' He ate sixty hard-boiled eggs, and I did the same with oysters."

Sam talked of the salmon he caught and the crabs he'd trapped. "It was food from the gods for those willing to take."

He spoke of trips to Alaska. They would hire bush pilots to take them to remote places to fish where the catching of them was so easy that after a while it became almost boring. "Dan there wasn't even a challenge."

His first time seeing Alaska was in a van after college, and he rode a ferry from Washington to get there.

I told him that his personal life of "riding a fairy" was more than I really needed or cared to hear about.

"Dan, I took four months off and explored places that I'd only heard or read about."

He told of those trips where he would stay in villages where there were only the indigenous people and even then very few.

Sam did anything and everything that he ever wanted to do, and along the way, the catching of fish was but another way to go to new places and meet new people. The aspect of fishing was something he had in common with those he met along the way. And the stories he heard and shared were his true love.

He talked about the transactions he'd made while at Coldwell. "Dan, I was amazed at how easy it was to get into the office of people who ran major operations. If I could get past the secretary, the head guy was only too willing to talk. It almost seemed as if he was happy to see someone. All his work was relegated to others, and I think that after a while it probably became boring."

Sam would find properties to sell and people to buy them. His transactions were not listed, and both the sellers and buyers dealt on a handshake if he could find the right buyer and seller at the right price. Contracts were drawn up after the deal was agreed upon.

I had told him that most of my contracts with my customers were on a handshake as well, though not at his level.

Sam had some pretty good sales. The old Sears and Roebuck catalogue warehouse he called a "gray elephant," a property that was not feasible for many in the commercial business. It had eight-foot ceilings, hardwood floors, and a million plus square feet. Sears workers would wear roller skates to fill orders. Sam sold it to an up-and-coming company called Starbucks. It was to become their headquarters.

"Dan, I could have bought their stock when they were making their first public offering, but who the hell would think that a coffee shop would go that far. They were only selling coffee after all!"

Another up-and-comer he showed an old Union Pacific Railroad depot to was Mark Cuban. Sam described him as "focused yet fun."

Sam was making his mark in the real estate world and some of those within his office liked to show off a bit. A salesman came in after closing a pretty good deal and flashed around his new Rolex.

The following week, everyone in the office was wearing a fake Rolex and no one could tell the difference.

"Dan, he was so pissed. To those not knowing, the only difference between his watch and the rest of ours was the price. That was the last time he wore that watch to the office."

Sam wanted to go out for breakfast and I was fine by that. We went down the road to a place he'd enjoyed in the past, Mangrove Mama's.

Along the way I noticed a sign that said "Skydiving" and told Sam that we should give it a try. He shook his head.

"No thanks, Dan."

I looked at him. "Sam, you are not even giving it any thought."

"There is nothing to think about. A plane is designed to take off, fly, land. Why the hell would I want to jump out of it?"

"Because you can, Sam. Because you're alive, and the adrenaline rush would be fun. Besides, if your parachute doesn't open, you would leave your family rich."

Sam told me that his parachute not opening wasn't a concern of his. "Dan, if you really want to know the truth, I'm afraid *yours* won't open. How the hell would I get back to camp?"

I said if that happened, the coroner would probably drop him off at the camp on his way by. "He might even let you take one last lap around the campground with me."

We walked into the restaurant and were seated. Sam commented to the waitress that he was glad to see she still worked here. (It had been a year since his last visit.)

They remembered each other and greeted each other by name. She said that she was actually now the owner.

Sam had been coming here for more than a few years and he had a way with people that they remembered him and his name and vice versa.

We ate our food and left. Sam with his "inside" information did manage to get the bill.

We headed back to camp and I told Sam that I'd be cooking clam sauce over linguine later, and if he didn't show up he'd have to find his morning coffee elsewhere.

"Dan, you said that you put the oo in food and the eff in chef, and I wouldn't want to miss out on that."

I was up front and getting some supplies, and I ran into Jonie. She asked me, "Is Sam all right?"

I wanted to know why she wanted to know, and she said that he'd taken a tumble on his bike.

On the way back I stopped by Sam's. "Sam, are you okay? I heard you took a spill."

"Where did you hear about that?" he said. "I only fell off my bike two minutes ago."

"What can I tell ya, Sam. Good news travels fast."

He said that his bike's wheel had gotten caught in a rut and he had fallen off, although he was fine.

Later that evening he stopped by with a bottle of rum and we ate and we drank. The food and the company was fun. I guess I must have walked him back home.

Chapter 23

I Just Want to Celebrate
Another Day of Living

The next morning, Sam and I were drinking our coffee when he asked me if I was okay. I really had no idea what he was referring to other than maybe the pounding in my head from a little too much rum the previous night.

"Sam, a couple of aspirin along with a couple of cups of coffee, as well as the enjoyment of your company, and I will be just fine."

Sam elaborated, "When you walked me back to my place last night, you took a pretty good fall."

"Sam, previously I doubted the reason for your fall as being your bike getting caught up in that rut. I think I found that same rut, and I am sorry for ever having doubted you."

We drank our coffee and Sam said that Joann was cooking a breakfast at her house this morning. I was expected as well.

Joann, being the matriarch of this establishment, the person that not only owned it but bought it when it was nothing more than a place where you pitched a tent wherever you felt like. There were no sites per se then, only vacant land from the front office and a few rooms above to the sea. It was not much more than a parking lot upon the coral. Along she came, and all that changed. It's now a slice of paradise for many.

Sam had told me their relationship had developed over the years that he'd been coming here, one based on friendship and a mutual respect for each other. They would spend time together talking or playing board games.

When I asked Sam if they had been "dating," all he'd say was that she was really someone he enjoyed being around. I could tell that he not only liked but admired this woman.

"Sam, I am in awe of the efficiency of this place."

"Dan, she knows what she wants, and she makes it happen. I would not want to go against her in any type of business. She was even an alternate for the Olympics as a target shooter. She is focused and determined. She runs this place as efficiently as any business I've ever seen."

He told of a time when Joann was hosting a dinner for the entire campground and one of her commercial-grade ovens broke.

"Dan, I only heard her side of the conversation. I think it was on a Saturday. She told this person on the other end of her phone that the oven had broken down and she needed someone to come fix it. There was a pause and she only said, 'This is Joann from the Fishing Lodge, and it will not wait until Monday.' She had barely hung up the phone when someone was there. I know she pays well, but she expects to be treated accordingly and will not tolerate anyone who will not give to her what she has paid for."

We were welcomed into Joann's house and were seated along with a few others. She served us a wonderful meal of various fruits, eggs, toast, and juice. She was a beautiful woman in both her looks and her demeanor. I would describe her as elegant. She knew everyone in camp by name, and I have never heard anyone say anything negative about her, not her employees nor the campers. She was loved by most and respected by all.

After breakfast, I walked along with Sam and left him at his camp to "dream" for a while and told him to stop by, that I was just going to be hanging around.

When he woke from his one-of-many daily hibernations, he came by and realized how cold it was, at least by the standards of the Florida Keys. The temperature had dipped into the fifties.

It's amazing just how quickly you become adapted to the climate you're in. Back home, the fifties in January would be a cause for celebration—open the windows and let the fresh air in; in the Keys it brought out the few warm clothes that people had brought along.

Sam went back to his camper and returned in a goofy orange hunting cap with the ear flaps pulled down. One of the Pirates (one-eyed Chuck) walked by with no shirt and a pair of shorts, and Sam and I figured he was trying to show the rest of the campsite just how tough those "blue-balled biker bastards from Wisconsin" were. I told Chuck to hold on a second.

As I said, Sam was looking a bit goofy in his hunting cap. I went inside my camper and returned with my winter hat and a camera and had Chuck take a picture of us.

Chuck told Sam to smile, and Sam said, "Sorry, Chuck, I can't smile on command." He later explained to me that it was one of the luxuries he was no longer afforded, thanks to Huntington's. I realized then how special this friendship was. Sam smiled and laughed often when we were talking, though it wasn't just his being polite. He couldn't even smile if he wanted to. It was something spontaneous that he couldn't control.

We talked for a while and when I asked about his dinner plans he said he'd been invited to Judy and Vaughn's place. Judy and Vaughn could often be seen walking around the campground with their son Greg, who I think had some form of autism. Whenever they'd walk by, Sam would say hi to Greg and once Greg said "Hi, Sam" in return. It was the only time I ever heard Greg speak.

I told Sam I'd be going over to Rudy and Sara's place, that they were hosting a dinner for a few people and they had invited me as well.

Later when I was passing Sam's place, I had my contribution for the dinner in hand: the same old bucket of popcorn I had brought to another party previously. Pretty sad, I know. I am a bachelor after all, and in my defense it was gourmet popcorn and four different varieties. I asked Sam if he'd like some.

"Yes I would. This is good. It's the same as you brought to Jonie's the other night."

I told Sam to "keep it down" because I didn't want it to get around that I was bringing leftovers. "Sam, why don't you grab a bowl and I'll leave ya some."

He said that he was fine, that he'd already had dinner and that he just wanted a little dessert.

"Sam, come on along over to Rudy's. You can be my date. You know everyone there."

"No thanks, Dan, I already had dinner over at Vaughn's."

We said our goodnights and I proceeded on my way. I was adding my popcorn to the various dinner entrees everyone else had contributed when someone tapped me on the shoulder. I turned around and it was Sam inquiring if he could have some more popcorn. I laughed. The thought of that popcorn was too much and he couldn't let it go.

Everyone there knew Sam. Rudy and Sarah, along with everyone else, insisted that Sam sit down and join in the feast. (To not accept was almost an insult to those offering.) Sam accepted and said he'd be right back. He returned with a bottle of wine (reserved I assume for such an occasion).

Room was made for Sam, and even though he claimed he was full and had already eaten dinner, he managed to eat everything that was set before him. Sam could always eat. His body in its state of constant motion must go through a lot of calories.

Sam was a good guest, talking and listening, and after dinner he pulled me to the side. "Dan, I've never crashed a party before."

I told him that he hadn't crashed, he'd been invited. His response was "No, Dan, I crashed that dinner party. I knew they would invite me."

Ya gotta love the guy.

Dinner done, conversations over, I walked Sam back to his place and continued on to my own.

Another day of life in the Keys.

Another day of living.

Chapter 24

Mr. Mike and the Bitten Coochie

The following morning, we were starting on our second pot of coffee when Sam asked about my previous night's writings. I told him that it was kind of falling by the wayside, a few notes was about all I could muster. The writing was going a bit slow, though I had at least come up with a new business venture for the two of us.

"Mr. Sam, what do you think of this one? Mouse flavored cat food!" I almost yelled it at him. "Ya gotta love it, Sam. Think about it! Cats not only love chasing mice, but they enjoy the capture and the torture of those poor little critters. They do seem to love their taste. All the cat food in the stores is flavored by nothing they actually get a thrill out of eating."

"If a cat loves you, it'll bring a mouse and lay it at your feet and meow till you acknowledge it and the gift it's laid before you. Their work, their diligence, placed before you is an offering for their love of you."

"Dan, you may be on to something here. If it's a hit, maybe we can follow it up with some cat-flavored dog food."

He was realizing all the possibilities when Mr. Mike, the ninety-plus-year-old, stopped by and interrupted the thoughts of our million-dollar enterprise. I waved him over and he sat down with us.

Sam and Mike started to talk about fishing and Sam told Mike how he used to fly fish for carp.

Mike looked at him as if he was totally nuts.

Sam responded, "Mike, the senses of carp are more acute than any fish I've ever tried to fool with an imitation insect or fly."

Mike shook his head in disgust. "What the hell are you talking about? The only thing you need to catch a carp is a hook and a piece of dead meat!" Mike scowled and Sam had a twinkle in his eye.

Sam said, "I used to fly fish for them in Michigan, where people would come from all over the world to try to catch them. They are referred to as the 'golden bonefish' among those who are looking for a challenge."

Mike looked at Sam and said he thought Sam was full of shit, and I (of course) had to add my two cents.

"You know, Mr. Mike, in some European countries carp is considered a delicacy. It is a prize catch."

Mike just looked at me. "And that's why they're foreigners. They eat funny food and talk funny."

I was amused by them throwing their barbs, jousting with each other.

It was obvious they were having fun, and their expressions said it all. Mike's scowl was a facade. He had a twinkle in his eyes and a smirk on his face that made it obvious (to me) they both liked and respected each other.

A fellow camper walked by and we said our hellos and exchanged a few pleasantries. After she had left, they both tried remembering her name. Not coming up with it, they both looked at me. I didn't know it either. They eventually did come up with it and both of them kept repeating it, willing it to their memories.

I was impressed. I think it was something they always did because it mattered to them. They were both advancing to a point most of us never will, whether with Mike's age or with Sam's Huntington's. I do believe it's why both maintained their mental faculties past the point most won't, Mike with his ninety-plus years and Sam twenty-plus years on with a disease that most succumb to much sooner.

They had both been in sales and they both realized the importance of developing relationships (though I believe it was because they really cared about people and it had nothing to do with any profit).

Mike left and another camper stopped by, but neither Sam nor I caught her name. She spoke in a very high tone, almost squeaky in its inflection, and her words were not really making a whole lot of sense. Maybe one in ten words could be understood.

She was probably well into her seventies and was staying a few campsites away with other people. By the way she was talking, I thought she must have some kind of problem, either because of her age or because of mental issues.

After ten minutes in her presence, Sam and I occasionally looked at each other in bewilderment, me raising my eyebrows and him shrugging his shoulders.

Finally she said in very clear voice that we both totally understood, "And that's why the church bells were ringing and that is the only reason." And she turned and left us.

Sam looked at me and he tried to come up with a reason for her nonsensical words. "Dan, I think she may be a little senile."

"You think, Sam, maybe just a little bit?" And the laughter that I was holding back suddenly came out. I had tried to contain it, as did Sam, though once the laughter began we were like a couple of kids that heard a fart reverberating against the wooden pews of a church. We couldn't stop.

"And that, Sam, is suppressed laughter at its finest!"

It was absolutely wonderful.

After a while, we attempted to act a bit more like adults (only after a while, and only a little). A fellow camper named Dan walked by, saying his good mornings.

Dan was not really a big talker, though he was a nice person. He and his wife Jonie had a place on the canal that most referred to as "The Riviera." It was a section along the canal leading into the campground from the ocean. It had electricity and a space for your boat right alongside your site, a place for those that had a few extra bucks to spend.

Sam said that Dan was always helping him if he needed to have things fixed, though he would never accept money.

"My toilet was leaking a few days ago and I asked Dan if he knew anything about them and I told him in no uncertain terms that the only way I would let him help me is if I could pay him.

"He agreed and pulled it apart, took a look at different things, and returned after a while with an O ring that he replaced. I tried to give him some money, but he refused, saying that the part was only a few cents. He had a friend who was staying with them for a few days and I told him that if he didn't take my money, the next time he went out fishing with his friend I would give his wife twenty dollars. He took my money."

After a while, Sam went about his way, as did I. Later in the day I saw him sitting at his table and sat down with him.

A most lovely woman walked by and began to ascend the stairs to the showers when Sam commented that she had such a nice tight little fanny that you could "chip a tooth on it." She was in her thirties and had a beautiful smile that all but radiated. She was also covered in tattoos.

She was half way up the stairs when she stopped and looked over at us and said, "Good morning, Dan."

I said, "Good morning, Sara. Be careful up there. They just had to call maintenance to help a woman that hadn't looked before she sat down. There was an iguana in the commode that bit her right on the coochie. They had to pry open its jaws with a screwdriver to get it to release."

She laughed and continued on her way.

Sam asked, "Who is that? She's beautiful, and what the hell's this about an iguana latching on to a woman's crotch. I didn't hear about that. I thought they only ate fruits and vegetables."

"Sam, when you were napping, I was out and about the campsite doing a little socializing and met a few other people, she being one of them. Sam, apparently iguanas like fish as well."

Sam ignored me and changed the subject. "Hey, Dan, there's a place I'd like to go to later for something to eat. They have really good pizza."

I agreed. Sam went into his camper for a nap, and I went out on the ocean to try to catch some fish, returning with a few for those back home.

Later Sam stopped by and wasted no time before talking about the pizza we would be going out for. "Dan, this place has the best pizza. It's a little hole-in-the-wall bar and there's not even a sign that lets you know it's there. In fact, the name of the place is No Name Pub."

He asked how I liked my pizza, and I told him, "Pepperoni, mushrooms, cheese. I like it all, Sam."

Sam said he liked anchovies. I'd never had anchovies before and I told him I'd give them a try.

We talked for a little while and Sam blurted out, "And garlic," in the middle of a conversation that had nothing to do with what we were talking about. Sam's mind was still on that pizza.

We went to the No Name Pub, which was just before "No Name Key" and after being seated and served, I had to agree that, even though I was from New York, which was home to a lot of Italians and great pizza, I was impressed.

Sam had gotten a side of anchovies that I tried on a slice. I decided that I too liked them.

Returning to camp, I dropped Sam off at his place and continued on to my own. Life can be wonderful when we share it with others and get outside our own selves. I crawled into my bed without considering my writings and immediately fell asleep.

Chapter 25

Sweet Dreams

I was deep in sleep, or I think I was, when I heard a knock at the door of my camper. It started out as a tap that kept on repeating: a few taps and then silence, a few more taps becoming a little louder until they became almost constant and louder still.

It had started out as soft, barely heard, as though it was part of a dream, until I realized that someone was actually at my door when the knocking grew louder and more persistent.

I heard the door of my camper open and someone whisper, "Danny, it's me."

Still not quite sure of anything, I gradually became aware of someone else's presence inside of my camper and moving toward me.

The whispered voice repeated, "Danny, it's me."

I had no idea who "it's me" was.

"It's me, Danny" was repeated in a voice so sensual, so sultry, that even being half asleep I felt myself becoming aroused by it.

"Hi, Danny. I thought I'd come by to keep you warm. I thought maybe you would like some company. I thought maybe, from the way you have been looking at me the past few days, you had the same thoughts, the same desires."

That someone came closer and then I felt her presence next to me. I heard what I thought were her clothes falling to the floor.

It was a starless night, the clouds obscuring any light from above, and I had none as well. The room was black. Whether my eyes were open or shut I saw the same thing: blackness.

The blankets keeping me warm were lifted from me, not only leaving me exposed but also my insecurities as she lay down next to me, pulling those sheets back over us. She whispered, "Shh."

It was all she said as I felt both her body and warmth.

"Danny, say nothing, please. Just lie here with me. I am only here to do what has been keeping me awake for too many nights. I've wanted you since we first met, since I first laid eyes on you, since the first time you said hello."

Her fingers had been upon my lips to keep me silent. It wasn't necessary. My own thoughts had left me without words.

She replaced her fingers with her lips and began teasing me. Her breath was warm and her breathing matched mine, heavy and gasping, mine maybe partially from my own insecurities. I lay there speechless, enjoying every sensation.

I wanted to express my uncertainty of being with someone unknown, yet I could say or do nothing other than to lie there.

I felt her breasts against my chest, her nipples moving against me, teasing my body. She pressed against my chest; her lips moved down from my neck to my chest, exploring, teasing.

Her hands grasped my penis as she moved further down my body with her mouth. As she

-240-

teased, I grew harder, and by the time her lips found what she wanted, I was past the point of caring or thinking about who it might have been. She took me into her mouth, my every nerve ending alive, flowing through me, rising, ready to explode. She became more aggressive. I felt her body quivering. She was pleasing herself as much as she was pleasing me as she took me even deeper.

"Oh, Danny!"

My eyes were still closed, and even through my ecstasy I knew something wasn't right.

That voice grew louder, "Oh, Danny, get your ass up."

It was Sam.

"SAM! What the fu—"

I sat straight up and smashed my head on the roof of my camper. (I'm talking my body here, not my penis—it was already there.)

"Oh, Danny, are you awake?"

I was in my camper still in bed. Alone!

I had been dreaming.

"Sam, give me a minute."

I think that I probably yelled it out and not in a nice way, "You have just interrupted the best sex I've had in a while!" I stepped outside, still a bit confused.

"Dan, I hope I didn't interrupt your sleep?"

"Sam, my sleep ain't no big deal. What you did interrupt was the most wonderful dream and the best sex that I've had in quite some time. Sam, I was right at the tail end of a dream with a most entertaining woman. I was about to release

-241-

an orgasm that would have blown the roof off my camper, and you were the reason my dream turned into a nightmare!"

Sam sat there and I didn't say anything else for a moment.

"Dammit, Sam, I was right there."

Sam feigned his concern. He tried to sound sympathetic. "I'm sorry, Dan."

When I was younger, my penis used to be awake before the rest of my body almost every day. As time has gone on, that has become less the case. It used to watch me shave each and every morning. Now, most mornings it watches me tie my shoes.

Sam laughed and did seem a little sorry. We talked of wet dreams and how they created the perfect scenario for sexual release. The mind tells us what we find attractive, and in a dream, the person you are with is perfect, even though I don't ever recall a face of that person. The mind is the sexual organ that drives everything, and in a dream it's pure ecstasy.

Sometimes it ends waking with a pup tent, an erection holding the blankets up. Trying to go back to sleep to finish that dream is always a waste of time. It never happens for me.

Sam said that he would leave if I would like to go back to bed. With him being the cause of my waking, and for way too long a part of my dream (it was only a brief moment), I wasn't in the least bit interested in completing it. In fact, I was afraid of ever going back to sleep. I didn't want to have another dream, not ever again.

Since he already had what he came for (my coffee pot, ready to go), I told him that I would be fine, that I might take matters into my own hands later while showering.

"Do you know what, Dan? My only release lately is either by my own actions or through my dreams. I still have those dreams a couple of times a month. I remember when I was young that if I didn't masturbate for a week or so, I would have those fantasies. I used to think that wet dreams were a gift from God. I really did believe that."

I was envious. Only a few of those dreams in my life had ever come to fruition, and my sexual partners lately were less frequent than twice a month.

While we sat there drinking our coffee, John, one of the Pirates, walked by. Almost every morning he would walk past, heading toward his morning shower or up front for a cup of coffee, and he always had his head bowed.

Sam and I both gave him a good morning. He returned in kind and continued on his way.

Sam said he liked John, and I said, "You know what I think?" I didn't wait for his response. "Every morning John walks by with his head hung low, not even looking around. He rarely acknowledges people in the morning, but by the afternoon you can't shut him up. I think he drinks so much the night before that he isn't ready to make eye contact with someone he may have offended, and by the afternoon he doesn't care.

"Sam, he drinks a bit too much, he gets a little too loud. He offends those that consider themselves the moral majority of the campground. He gives the gossipers someone to talk about because they have someone they can look down upon to make themselves feel better about how good they are, and they leave the rest of us alone. What's not to like about him?

"He's about as harmless as anyone I've ever met. He laughs often, and sometimes his laugh is almost a giggle. He's one hell of a cook. He can take whatever is in his fridge, mix it together, and turn it into something really good that he'll share with all. I have never heard him say a bad thing about anyone.

"Sam, last year John was on his scooter and he and his bike both went down. He must have found that rut in the road that snuck up on us. He was pretty bloodied up and wound up going to Emergency, needing a few stitches. The next day I asked him how he was doing and he told me that he was just fine. He told me about the first time he had gone down on a motorcycle when he was fourteen years old. He said that his father took one look at him and said, 'Boy, if you're going to be stupid, you'd better be tough.' He said that he just got tough.

"I think maybe John is just checking on gravity from time to time to make sure it still works. After his fall, his motorcycle was in need of some work. I gave him a ride into town the following day and later on he brought me by a plate of Wisconsin cheese and some jerky that he had made. I said that wasn't necessary and he only said that he was cleaning his refrigerator and had to get rid of a few things.

"What's not to love about him? He gives the fools of the campground someone to talk about and I would rather it be him than me. He is an easy target for those that love to point at others rather than looking in the mirror.

"I think that from here on out, anytime I see someone staggering about after a few too many cocktails, I'll refer to them as doing the Johnny Red as in that Scotch named Johnny Walker Red. I know I've done the Johnny Red more than a few times down here myself. My opinion of him is I love the guy."

It was Sam's turn to tell me his thoughts.

"Dan, John has been coming down here for almost as long as me, maybe even longer, and he oftentimes stops by my place just to talk. You are right insofar as it's probably not first thing in the morning, but after his coffee or maybe even later. He is always ready to talk. I really do like him. He's really very intelligent and well read. He keeps up on everything and can carry on an informed conversation about almost any subject."

I told Sam not to bother asking about a restaurant for breakfast. I had bought some curds and whey that I thought might agree with the diet he was on, and I had a few breakfast steaks in my cooler.

I fired up my outdoor grill and put an iron skillet over the flames. I put a little olive oil into the pan as well as some diced up potatoes, peppers, and onions. I had a pan next to it that I fired up with some butter, and once it was really hot, threw the steaks on, blackening the outside and searing the juices inside, leaving them rare, yet charred on both sides. A few eggs over medium, some burnt bread, and breakfast was ready to be served.

I cut up Sam's steak, handing him over the whole concoction, and the rest was up to him.

We ate and One-eyed Chuck stopped by and said hello. We talked for a few minutes and he told us that John had quit drinking and that they were thinking of starting a pool to see just how long he'd last. I asked him if it was by the hour or the day. He laughed and continued on his way.

Sam said that if I wasn't busy later that day, he was hoping I wouldn't mind giving him a ride a ride up to Marathon, a little to the north or maybe east of us. I am lost as far as the compass is concerned down here. I only know the mainland is north of us and Key West is further south from the mainland and toward the west, and I was somewhere in between.

"Sam, I am at your service. I am your chauffer for the day."

"Dan, I need to send a few things to my sister that I won't be able to get on a plane. There's a UPS store there that will ship my stuff back home."

I didn't ask why he needed to ship his stuff and fly home. Maybe I just didn't want to know. He headed back to his place for his beauty nap.

Sitting at my table a little while later, I saw John walking by sipping from a glass and yelled out, "Hey, John, I thought you had quit drinking."

"It's only wine, Dan. It doesn't count. It's doctor's orders. It helps with my constipation."

A while later I was walking about the camp when I saw Sam at his table and I stopped by to say that the beauty rest thing wasn't working. He paid me no mind.

He said that his sister had found a place in Michigan not far from her that was independent living. "Both she and my family, as well as some of my friends, researched different places and they all agreed that it seems a good fit for me. Dan, I'm not really looking forward to this, but I'm told it's a really nice place."

Sam said that it was a Catholic facility and he only hoped that it wasn't run by the same nuns he had back in grade school. "Dan, I really don't think my ass could take any of those yardstick spankings anymore."

I said that he just might enjoy having his buttocks turned rosy red by a stern-looking woman standing over him. "Sam, some guys actually pay good money for something like that."

"You know what, Dan, maybe you're right, but one of my biggest concerns is the social aspect. These people are all old and I need to socialize."

"Sam, it's been my experience that a lot of older people only want someone to talk to because they have a lifetime of memories they long to share with anyone willing to listen. If nothing else, you are a good listener, and I think you may have people standing in line trying to fill your ears with their memories of days gone by."

Sam said he was hoping one of the old farts would adopt him and look out for him.

He only had to get a few things together, if I still was up to giving him a ride.

"I left an opening on my calendar just for you, Sam."

Seeing his boxes sitting there, I knew that he had been, for lack of better words, "packing for his last trip." I was in awe of how stoic he remained, how he acted as if it was just another obstacle in the road that had been paved by his ancestors before him, a road that he had foreseen and had anticipated.

The only outward indication was his movements were a bit more pronounced, and the only reason I noticed was because we'd spent so much time together. I'm sure no one else in this place would have noticed.

My eyes began to well with tears, and if I had been alone, I wouldn't have held them back.

I wasn't about to be outdone by Sam. I had to turn away for a moment to try to remain composed. One of the things I do like about myself is that I am not so macho as to be worried about crying, though in this case it wasn't about me. Hell, I cry at movies.

We loaded Sam's belongings into my truck and went to the UPS store. I told him that I wanted to go back to that happy-hour place for a few Margaritas, some oysters, and that undercooked tuna we'd had before, but only if I could pay for it. Otherwise, I would be dropping his sorry ass back at his site and he would have to eat that chicken shit salad he kept in his fridge.

Sam agreed and I told him to not even try getting cute with the waitress and grabbing the bill. I would be buying, or he too would have a UPS stamp on his ass and heading north.

Chapter 26

Doctor of Death

The next morning arrived and Sam and I said our morning hellos as we sat down with our cups of coffee. His demeanor was not the same as I was used to. He was usually upbeat and ready to welcome a new day with a smile and conversation. It was obvious that something was bothering him and he confirmed it by asking me so matter-of-fact if I'd ever heard about that doctor that had helped people commit suicide. I had a feeling it was something Sam had been thinking about.

"I do remember him and I think that his name may have been Kevorkian. He was known as 'the doctor of death.'"

I'm not sure that Sam even heard me. He continued expressing his thoughts. "Do you know what, Dan? The last person Dr. Kevorkian helped leave this world with a little dignity was a person just like me, someone who had not only lived a full life and had a mind cognizant enough to realize that the body was done and was ready to move on, but who did not have the strength nor the ability to end it for themselves. Kevorkian helped people. He did for people what they wanted to do for themselves but couldn't.

"Kevorkian was a fucking idiot! He wanted to go to trial. He actually filmed what he did, so in essence he built a case against himself. I can't believe just how stupid he was. Kevorkian was really a fucking fool."

There was no real emotion in Sam's voice, though he seemed a little saddened as he spoke.

"Sam, you've contemplated suicide?"

He continued talking as if he hadn't heard me. "What he did, Dan, was help someone move on peacefully, with a little dignity. Not just someone, but lots of people. There is a difference between living and just being alive. Kevorkian helped those who knew they were no longer truly living. There comes a time in life when doctors seem to go against nature to see just how long they can keep a body at play. The more insurance someone has, the longer they keep them going. What's sad is that with all those who believe in a God, they still want to keep a dying person alive. It's almost as if they are playing God by thinking they are doing His will, for what fucking possible reason?

"Dan, there are those who truly believe that there's an afterlife. Don't you think that they would want to go there and embrace the rewards they think awaits them? Yet for whatever reason, we have to be kept alive through medicine and kept plugged in, and the only ones who benefit are the insurance companies or the hospitals."

Sam said that he had heard drowning was peaceful.

I loved busting Sam's balls, but the reason we spoke so openly was because we both knew when to listen, when to comment, and I suppose this was my time to shut up and listen. But just what could I possibly say?

We sat there for a while, neither saying anything, when Sam asked me if I believed in God or a life after death.

I pondered his question. I wanted to make sure he even wanted a response, and when he just sat there, I figured it was my opening to talk.

"Sam I remember our priest coming into the classroom. It was probably the fourth grade. He spoke with our (nun) teacher and the only thing I remember him saying is 'None of you still believes in Santa Claus, do you?' Of course we all agreed, though a little of my innocence was lost that day. Children should lose their innocence in their time, not when someone else wants them to. It was that priest and his God that lost that day. I still believe in Santa but not his God, and no one has ever killed in Santa's name. Sam, if you really want an answer I do have one."

I looked at him and he just sat there. He looked as though he was still contemplating things that I didn't want to know about.

"Sam there are a bunch of idiots out there that pose hypothetical questions with no right or wrong answers, one of them being, 'Is the glass half-empty or half-full?' It's a dumb question because it's both, half-full and half-empty. Some idiot in front of a classroom is trying to kill time with a bunch of nonsense so they can get into our heads—although if I might add, it really depends on what's in the glass."

Sam just sat there.

"If it's a beer, Sam, it's half-empty. If it's a glass of medicine, it's half-full. I suppose the real answer is that it's full: half with whatever and the other half with air."

If there were two other people in a room, Sam was social. We had both become okay with saying nothing.

Sam looked up; Sam always listened. You just had to pause for a second or two and he would respond.

"Dan, what's half a glass of water got to do with a God?"

"I really don't know, Sam. I can never imagine a divine entity being thirsty. I guess if there's a God like religions think of him, those that follow quench His thirst with the blood that they spill in His name."

I paused for a minute and continued, "Sam, if you would have the decency to let me continue without your interruptions, you will see just where I'm going."

He sat there with an amused look.

"Teachers pose questions with no right or wrong answers. Now, Samuel, I ain't a college edicated person like you is, though I'm a thinkin' it might be philosophy? Irregardlessly, Sam, the one question I do like that has been posed to many a person is 'If a tree in the forest falls and there is no one around to hear it fall, does it still make a sound?' I know it really is a dumb question, but some smart person came up with it, probably a graduate from MSU, maybe even a professor there."

He looked at me again with an amused expression and I knew I had him.

"All right, Sam, I am sorry for my roundabout way of giving you an answer. Of course that tree makes a sound, and I know it for a fact! In other words, Sam... goddammit, sometimes you just gots to believe! Sam, I do believe in something past this life as much as I do know that a tree falling does make a sound."

I also said that I didn't think any religion had any concept of "God's" will.

"Sam, I do believe something designed this universe, and I am just amazed that the fools of this world think that God needs their help in keeping it right. To be in awe is one thing, to be righteous is fine, but those that think they are 'holier than thou' are only looking to be admired.

"I do think that there is something that has a hand in this thing we call life. I'm a thinkin' that it just might be a power greater than us, but it isn't to be found in no manmade religion."

"I once read a quote that has been attributed to Albert Einstein when he was questioned about his belief in God. The only thing he could say was 'I do not know if there is a God. The only thing that I do know is that energy never dies, it only changes forms.'

"Sam, one of the greatest minds of our time knew, he *knew* for a fact, that though our body ceased, our energy would continue on. Sam, something in us will live on.

"When my father was dying, we kept him at home and out of the hospitals with some help from visiting nurses. As my dad's time to move on came closer, most of my family was there, and one time he was lying in his bed and my sister Sue was with him. He looked at her and said, 'Tillie is here and she wants me to go with her. She's telling me it's time.'

"That's all he said to her, Sam: 'It's time.'

"Tillie was my father's sister, who had already passed on, and even with my sister's encouragement telling him to go with Tillie, he still wouldn't leave.

"Sam, I have no idea how hard it had to be to tell someone you love so much that it's time to move on, yet my sister Sue still did.

"The next time my dad said 'Tillie's here,' my sisters Cindy and Sue were cleaning him up after he had shit himself. They had sent me to the store for some clean-up supplies. This time he didn't need any encouragement. He crapped his drawers, and while my sisters were cleaning him up, he left us. I guess it was his final way of saying goodbye to them."

I told Sam I knew that scientists had explanations and religions as well. The only thing I knew for sure was my father's sister Tillie was waiting to show him the other side—and that falling trees still made sounds whether or not someone was present.

"Fuck a bunch of scholars, Sam. Sometimes, ya just gots to believe."

I also shared with him my writings of the previous year, or rather my experience in discovering that I had a creative side.

"Sam, I'd never written anything before that article, and suddenly I fashioned myself an author writing a book. Within a few short weeks I had completed it, at least in rough form.

"It was as if that story was writing itself. I would have a thought, and it would turn into a sentence, a paragraph, a chapter, almost as if I wasn't even involved. Thoughts would come to me with such force, such clarity, almost as if I was merely a conduit that flowed through to the paper. I would go to sleep, and a short while later be awake with my paper and pen, the pages being filled with words and thoughts so fast that I was almost unable to keep up with them. I would be in the shower and have to step out to write my thoughts down. It was weird, it was strange, it was fun. It was totally beyond me.

"Upon leaving and driving home, I was still writing, and the notes and thoughts were being written even while driving. It got to the point where I had to pull over at a rest stop. I couldn't even drive. I was living inside my mind, and it was totally beyond my comprehension or capability to deal with. In that rest stop I tried to sleep, but I had a revelation or epiphany or something way beyond my understanding.

"Suddenly I was in the presence of God, THE God, Sam, not the guy on the cross, not the mean-looking guy in a white robe and flowing beard that stood over the clouds with a look of menace and that ruled the universe. It was *my* God, and I only felt the presence of a blinding power of pure knowledge. Sam, in that moment I knew there was a God, and whatever my creativity caused within my mind, it allowed me to experience not only the genius that lies dormant in all of us but a taste of the beauty that I do believe we all will be in the presence of someday."

I told him that all those writings of the previous year I had thrown away because I had seen that fine line between genius and insanity, and it scared me. I wasn't sure I could handle it, though now, reflecting on it, I know that creativity is a strange thing if you aren't ready.

"Sam, when I write, I relive my past. It all comes back to me. I enjoy writing even though it's kinda strange."

I showed him a poem I'd written that I thought might explain some of the things I had gone through while writing. (Yes, I had even discovered poetry.)

Teardrops To Be Read

I cry at night from this gift within
As my life flows through a pen.
Both tears of joy and sorrow
As I live my past again.
It's my teardrops that are read.

I also told him that my story now consisted of only a few notes I had managed to salvage, along with the thoughts of that story that were still in my mind.

Sam had had a lot of years not only to contemplate his death, but to contemplate life in the hereafter, and I think, by his expression and body language, that he had found a little bit of solace in my thoughts and in my answer to his question of what I believed.

He didn't respond, which left me more than a little excited. Yes! I had finally left him speechless!

We sat there for a little while, then Sam decided to explain why he had shipped his belongings home. "Dan, I got pulled over not too long ago by a police officer. Someone had called in that someone was on the road and drunk, driving erratically. That someone driving badly was me. When the officer approached me, he told me why I was being pulled over. After a few minutes of talking, he knew that I hadn't been drinking, but he told me that he had to write me up. He said that I'd have to be retested to see if it was safe for me to be on the roads. Otherwise, I had thirty days left to drive. Dan, I knew I would have to jump through so many hoops that I wouldn't be able to keep my license. My drive down here was the last time I'll ever drive."

It was another step in the road that Sam had known was coming. He lost his driving rights and some more of his independence that day. I was in awe of how stoic he was in talking of moving into "independent" living.

Everyone that knew him wondered if he was okay driving, yet when I saw him ride that bicycle, with his body going every which way yet still maintaining the course, I knew he was a lot better than many a woman driver (kidding folks).

Sam sold his van to Jeb, the son of Brenda, daughter to Joann (you figure it out). He had listed his camper on the Internet. Someone came down from Miami to look at it and upon seeing it never even tried to negotiate a better price. He immediately gave Sam a check even though Sam said he still needed it for the duration of his stay. The man said the check was good and to cash it. He was okay with the wait. Sam had that effect on people; they just trusted him.

It was my turn to be left without a response. Sam was one tough individual who had spent many years knowing where his road led, but I was still amazed at how he just accepted it. I was in awe at his dignity in the way he handled what to so many would be so hard.

Sam was ready for a nap and I went about my way.

Later that day, Sam stopped by to tell me that tonight he would be buying dinner at a local place that had tacos for sixty-nine cents during happy hour and drink specials as well. He said he'd be buying me two tacos and a beer, maybe two beers if I was nice to him. How the hell could I refuse?

We sat at the bar and ordered a couple of beers when Sam said that two beautiful women had just walked in and were checking us out. When I turned to look, they were walking away, and Sam proclaimed, "That's the last time I will ever tell you to look over at a woman. As soon as they saw you turning toward them, they ran off into the back!"

We ate our food and headed back to the campground, calling it a night.

Chapter 28

Cry Uncle

The following morning came, as did Sam. We sat there drinking our coffee and talked about nothing that really mattered. (Though how often does anyone say anything that really matters longer than the time it takes to say it?)

After a short while, I decided to cook up some breakfast without bothering to ask Sam if he was hungry. It was a question I already knew the answer to: Sam was always hungry. He seemed to burn up a lot of calories.

When it came to wondering if you might be a good cook, Sam was a chef's dream. He never complained, only espoused the wonders of the foods set before him.

I scrambled up some eggs, fried some chopped up potatoes and onions in a little olive oil and grilled some tortillas over charcoal until they had charred a little.

I put the grilled tortillas in a fry pan and put the whole concoction together along with a little cheddar cheese until it started to melt, put another tortilla on top, and upon it all I put some salsa. I cooked up a few and set them on a plate, slicing them like a pie, and handed Sam over a few pieces.

Sam sat there eating and proclaimed how wonderful my cooking was.

"I'll say what I've said before, Sam. I put the eff in chef and the oo in food."

Sam smiled and kept on eating. "Dan, this really is wonderful."

My food is simple. It is as basic as it gets, yet with Sam everything was a marvel. Sam just enjoyed; Sam never complained about anything or anyone. Hell, I think I could have given him a turd sandwich with mustard and he wouldn't have complained.

The wind must have been blowing in just the right direction—or maybe it was the wrong direction. My neighbor must have had his nose in the air and followed it to my campsite. He had never stopped in before, nor had I ever invited him. We had talked previously (more than a few times), but it was only casual banter, in passing or up front at the liar's bench.

He called himself "Uncle," and that's how he introduced himself to everyone and anyone he met. It's what everyone knew him as. He wished us both a good morning and said that my food "smelled absolutely wonderful and it looked just as good as it smelled." He asked if he might try some. I was wishing that this campground allowed dogs so that I could serve up a turd sandwich for him.

I love cooking and sharing with others, though I do it with those I like, and those I like I readily share everything I have with. I always have a cooler of beer available to those people.

I dislike those that invite themselves and never seem to offer anything in return. I like most people, and even though I'd been camping next to this person for a while, I still hadn't gotten a good feeling about him.

I took a slice of my tortilla breakfast special and cut it in half and let him have his taste. He began to talk of the inheritance he had gotten and how he was enjoying it. His parents had died, and basically he was blowing their life savings on the things he never worked hard enough to get on his own.

He now had a goofy-looking motorcycle with two wheels on the front and one in the rear. Every time he tried to take off, he would stall the engine at least a couple of times, if not a dozen. It had been bought, thanks to his parents' savings. He said that he had finally gone to the Philippines on a vacation he'd only dreamt about, again because of his parents' lifelong labor, and I can only assume they were frugal in their spending.

He spoke of how beautiful both that country and its people were, and he made a comment about the children that struck me as totally not right.

After he left, I looked at Sam. "Am I wrong or did he just say that the kids over there were really wonderful if their parents weren't around?"

Sam looked at me and said that he had indeed heard the same thing. Sam always thought that whenever kids were around, Uncle seemed to be a little more friendly. He also bragged about his Bible studies classes that he taught to children and the Boy Scouts and how he just loved the children. I could only think of one reason someone would want to get a child away from their parents, and I didn't like my thoughts. He left me feeling a bit uneasy about him.

Sam and I finished our meal and we both sat there and kind of contemplated "Uncle Sam." It's not a good thing to think that someone liked children for more than the way they laughed and their pure innocence and their unadulterated view of the world.

Sam and I parted ways, he to explore the inner regions of his mind (or rather to stare at the back of his eyelids) for a moment or a couple of hours.

I had a lot of things I wanted to do. Two hours later, when Sam stopped back, I was in my lounge chair thinking about a whole lot of things I still wanted to do.

Sam had mentioned a few days ago a "block party" dinner later that evening and he reminded me of it before he headed back into the campground to visit others.

This block party was a get-together for the whole camp put on by a few of the campers. A part of the campground was sectioned off for the night's festivities. You bring a dish to pass, as well as your own drinks, and for the most part, the rest of the fools within this place—me being one of them—will provide much of the entertainment. Two of the hosts were Ron and his wife Bonnie.

Sam's presence had already been requested at Ron and Bonnie's table, and I suppose by this time that Sam and I were just considered "together" for lack of a better term. He had been told to bring me along.

"Finally, Sam, I am beginning to see a benefit to this friendship." Little Joanie pulled me aside and said that Sam would be at the head of the opening of the buffet line, and I began to think that maybe I should be a little nicer to Sam.

I wondered how well that would go over with the "vultures," the name I referred to those that always seemed to be the first in line once the buffet opened because they circled the head of the table, carrying on a conversation until the table and food was ready to be served. The closer it came to that time, the closer they got to the food until you could hear them say, "Oh my, we are first in line."

It was always the same people, and they made sure their plates were full of what they wanted to the point of overflowing.

Ron stood up to say a prayer and invoked the name of his Lord and Savior Jesus Christ. He thanked his God and the heavens for their blessings that had been bestowed upon him and all of us (it was nice) and asked that those still suffering could be helped.

I thought of those I knew in my own life that were suffering, family and friends up north freezing their asses off and hoping that the sun would eventually show up along with a few days in a row over thirty degrees.

Ron was a good man, and just as the buzzards were about to rip their claws into the feast of the carcass that was spread out before them upon the tables, he announced that Sam Catalano would be starting the procession.

You could almost see the pain it caused them, having to retract their talons and put their tongues back in their mouths. Some of them even had to grab a napkin to wipe the saliva running down their faces.

It was an odd feeling to have to part the seas of those that had worked so hard, trying to seem as if they were carrying on a conversation as they anticipated their reward, while I moved Sam and myself to the front.

I'd been to a few dinners before, but I had always waited till the line died down a bit. I was in awe of just what my fellow campers had brought. There are a lot of good people in this campground, and many of them share foods they are proud of cooking. I had never seen it before; the vultures always took the tastiest parts of the feast for themselves. Much of it was picked clean long before the end of the line, where I usually was.

It was a sight to behold, and I did sample a few of their wares, though it was Sam's plate I was filling and I couldn't hold two and fill them both at the same time. I let the line die down before feeding myself and still managed to find a few scraps that weren't picked clean off those bones. Still, there was plenty of food even with half the serving dishes emptied. Ron and Bonnie were wonderful people and the most gracious of hosts.

Dessert was brought to the buffet table. Joann (the owner) brought Sam what she herself had made. I had to get my own.

When I returned and asked where Sam was, I was told that he had gone to the restroom. I knew better. Sam had headed back to his place. It was an easy excuse to escape. To say he was going to retire would have left himself open to everyone telling him not to.

I stayed a bit longer, and soon after, I went back to my place as well. I made no excuses, I just left.

* * *

(Uncle didn't live far from me back home and made the local headlines. He had been arrested, and to avoid trial, he pleaded guilty to sexual conduct with a child. I sent that article to the campground, and he is no longer allowed there.)

Chapter 29

MSU

The next morning came and I began our conversing.

"Hey, Sam, I've been awake half the night trying to come up with an idea that between your corporate mind and my newfound creativity we can work on together, and I've come up with one that I think is a good one. I even have a target group of people. If you remember that guy with the three sixes, then I think this one will fit right in.

"Sam, there seems to be an awful lot of people out there planning for the end of the world, or the Apocalypse. Armageddon is at hand after all, and the Mayan calendar never went past 2012 and December of that year. Survivalists are preparing for it all, but I have to wonder if they really believed the world was ending, why they wouldn't just enjoy the little time we have left instead of preparing for being the only ones to survive.

"Anyways, Sam, if we got a whole bunch of Ziploc bags, I think we could turn around and sell them to people as dehydrated water!"

Sam didn't comment and I figured maybe he didn't quite comprehend the cost versus profit ratio and what a great idea it was. Or maybe he wasn't quite awake yet. It would probably hit him later and he would realize just what a genius I was.

We sat there, drinking our coffee, and Sam asked if I followed any sports. He mentioned his alma mater, Michigan State University, and probably the only sport he cared about, Michigan State University football. Professional sports really didn't interest him.

"Sam, in Rochester we've got baseball with the Red Wings and a hockey team with the Amerks. I believe there might also be a soccer and a lacrosse team, though I only follow baseball and hockey and even then I'm not one of those people that live and breathe because of a game played by adults. It's just fun.

"What I like about minor league teams is the players are still living their dream. They are still reaching for the stars. They have a goal, unlike so many that make it to the majors and couldn't care less about the fans, or for that matter, the game. Not only that, Sam, but in the minor leagues, fans don't hate the other team or their fans. It's just fun and the boos are a part of it. You can take kids and you are safe wearing an opponent's jersey."

Sam told me of Michigan State and the rivalry with the University of Michigan. "Dan, we had a lot of fun while in school, and the rivalry still continues even into adulthood for probably anyone that went to either school.

"My dentist was a graduate of UM. He's a good friend of my brother. They get together almost every week. My brother is an MSU grad like me and went to see this dentist as a patient. He needed a few new caps on his front teeth. This guy took an imprint and put a couple of temporary caps on his teeth until the permanent ones arrived. He gave my brother a mirror to check out the temporaries. One tooth had a U on it and the other had an M. My brother did not smile for two weeks."

I told Sam that it would be a lot more fun if all fans were that way. "We should enjoy the game and the rivalry. Once it gets to the majors, we are only dollar signs for the players. For the most part, those that idolize their 'heroes' are not even known by those they worship."

I said that I thought that his dentist was acting awful childish to stoop to such a base thing at his brother's expense and that he sounded like my kind of people. I loved it.

Sam kept on talking about his Alma Mater. "Dan, I remember being in the showers with a bunch of other people, one of them being a football player. He was already a star, at least at the college level. We were taking a shower at the same time with a bunch of other guys. He had a dick that almost reached the floor. He had a trunk that an elephant would have been proud of. He dropped a bar of soap and I half expected him to pick it up with his cock. I wasn't even embarrassed looking at it. I just couldn't imagine anyone having what amounted to a third leg."

Sam mentioned his name but I won't. I told him that I really didn't care who it was, though it was probably not a rumor he would deny.

I asked Sam if he felt like going fishing with me and he said that he didn't really think my boat was designed for him, no seats and a little small for the ocean. He knew that he would get bounced around a lot. In fact, he said that it would beat the shit out of him.

"Dan, I've gone out with guides a lot of times down here. I'd fish for tarpon with a fly rod and caught more than a few. It got to the point that I would wish they'd jump the hook and get off. I found that the challenge was in presenting the fly and getting them to bite. I just don't have it in me anymore to take all the effort involved to get one to the boat, or any fish for that matter."

The last few times Sam went out he said the guide would hang on to the back of Sam's belt because he was afraid that Sam would fall overboard. Sam's disease had progressed to the point that others were more concerned with the risks he took than he was. Sam was too busy living to worry about dying.

I told him I wanted some poached eggs for breakfast and if he wanted to fill my ears with any more of his bullshit, he'd have to eat my food, or he'd have to leave: poached eggs on rye toast with some fried up potatoes and a side of bacon. How could anyone refuse an offer like that?

We ate and a fellow camper named Wyatt stopped by. I had seen a fishing chair that Wyatt had in front of his place, a chair designed to be bolted to the floor of a boat. That would give Sam no excuse to not fish with me. It had been there for a while so I asked Wyatt if he wanted to sell it. I told him it was for Sam. Wyatt wasn't ready to sell, but said I could take it for as long as I wanted.

We were sitting around talking when another camper (Bob) stopped by and wanted to know if we knew which way the wind was blowing that day because he was considering going out onto the ocean.

Wyatt took one look at him and said, "How long have you been coming here?"

Bob said it had been for quite a few years, and Wyatt told him to turn around and look at the weather vane on the roof of the office not that far away and in plain view. It had always been there.

"I used to know it was there," Bob said.

"What the hell do you mean you used to know?"

"I used to do a lot of drugs, and since I quit I don't remember things so well."

"Well maybe you should start doing drugs again," Wyatt suggested.

Campers are a fun bunch of people. How the hell could you not love them? Most of those down here were getting up in their years and some just told it the way it was, though I've a feeling age has nothing to do with those that express their thoughts openly. I often wonder why we all don't.

If we don't like someone, that's all right because we are all different. I can't figure out why so many pretend to people's faces to like them, yet when their backs are turned, express true feelings to others. If I don't like someone, I can't pretend I do.

Everyone went on their way. I told Sam that I liked Wyatt even with his gruff demeanor. Sam agreed.

Sam was ready for a nap and I was headed out to catch a few fish. He had a prior engagement for dinner.

Chapter 30

10 Past 6:30

I found myself lying in bed, fully awake, and took a peek at the clock on my phone. It was 5:00 A.M. After twenty minutes or so of hoping to go back to sleep, I got up and put on a pot of coffee. By six I thought, *what the hell*, and brought my pot of coffee over to Sam's.

I knocked on his door. "Hey, Sam, get your lazy ass up. I'm bored and you have the rest of eternity to catch up on your sleep."

He stuck his head out the door. "What time is it, Dan, 6:30?"

"No, Sam, it's ten after."

"So it's 6:40."

"Well, no. l suppose in that case, it's thirty before."

"So it must be 6:10. Why the hell didn't you just say so in the first place?"

I told him to put some clothes on before coming out. It was warm and he'd have no excuse for his little weenie being cold and shriveled. He said he would be wearing shorts long enough that nothing would be hanging out. When he came out, he had shorts that went down to his knees.

"Sam, why are you wearing those long things? If you only needed to cover your manhood, I figured you'd be wearing Speedos and not even need the elastic around the legs."

He'd brought his coffee cup with him. We sat, and he wondered, "To what do I owe the pleasure of your presence at my residence at this time of the morning?"

"Sam, you said you'd be buying breakfast this morning and I wanted to make sure you didn't sneak off while I wasn't looking."

Jonie (of Jonie and Dan) walked by and asked how we were doing. Sam said that now that she was here, he was doing wonderful. "Jonie, I hope your husband doesn't come by with those dark clouds that always seem to follow him."

She continued on her way with a smile that Sam seemed to bring to anyone that took the time to say hello.

Another camper walked by, saying his good mornings. After he had passed, Sam asked if I knew his name.

All I could remember was his last name, Star. "We've spoken before, and between his size and personality I've thought of calling him The Big Easy, though with his last name, The Big Dipper seems more appropriate. He really seems like nice people. He's down to earth, got a quick wit and is fun. That guy has been coming down here with his parents since he was a teenager. He refers to the area past the fish cleaning station as 'The Dark Side.' He said that to walk into that section after 5:00 P.M. could result in both the loss of time and memory by the time you made it out.

"One time he hung out with some people he described as hillbillies, and he doesn't remember anything other than he woke up a day and a half later on a picnic table. It seems those hillbillies had some moonshine."

A few cups of coffee later, I took my morning shower and we went to Consuelo's. He didn't fill up as much on the main course of *huevos rancheros* so that he was able to eat his flan, which he said was wonderful.

Sam had mentioned that some friends of his were coming down early that afternoon to spend a couple of days. Nine of his childhood sweethearts were coming, friends of his from as far back as elementary school to his college years, some from as far away as Hawaii, some from just up the coast of Florida.

"Dan, I've known these guys since I was a whole lot younger and we've remained close. Everyone's wives or girlfriends not only accept our spending time together, but they want us to."

He said that they would get together a few times a year and had done so since college, even though they were scattered all about the country. Apparently they had all been relatively successful. One of his friends was a high-ranking official in the FBI, several were real-estate developers, whether it be homes or shopping malls. One was the intellectual of the bunch, an environmental lawyer who had represented some very high-profile cases against some major corporations. Sam said that if he had been a criminal lawyer, he would probably have been a millionaire a whole bunch of times over.

When they arrived, I met them, then went about my way. Sam's friends were here to spend time with him. I'd get on with my half-assed writing attempts and do a little fishing, although upon reflection I wish I had stayed.

Chapter 31

Wee Bonnie

I was awake. I had been for quite some time, drinking my coffee.

Just me, no one else...

Alone.

All by myself.

Something wasn't what it should have been. Something was missing. As the caffeine began to kick in, I realized that Sam was missing. I headed over to his place.

He had probably stayed up late with his friends, but I had a pot of coffee to finish and needed a little help. He would understand. After all, the nuns did teach us it was a sin to waste. I figured Sam had slept long enough. I brought along my pot of coffee. He'd still be awake early. Sam liked his bean juice.

I knocked on his door and said in a loud whisper, "Sam, get your lazy ass up."

Okay, maybe it was not so much of a whisper, more of a loud demand. If I woke his neighbors, I figured that having a class act like Sam for a neighbor, they could put up with me for a moment or two. They were on vacation and really shouldn't have a schedule that needed to be kept. If I did indeed awaken them, then they had another month or so to catch up on the sleep I had deprived them of.

Sam had left me alone the morning after spending a day and night with my nephew, but what can I say, other than maybe I am not as classy a person as Sam. After all, I had left him alone with his friends for a day or so, and I kinda missed his sorry, ugly ass.

Sam was awake, though not yet up and about. It took him a little bit (with persistent knocking on my part) to finally find his way to the door.

We drank a few cups of coffee, and after a little while his friends started showing up and I left him to be with those he loved and who loved him.

I went back to my campsite, got into my truck, and headed into town to get my day's supply of bait.

The sign on the front of the bait shop may have said, "Open at 7:00 A.M." In Keys' time that meant 7:00 give or take.

I had grown accustomed to it in the little time I had spent here. I truly enjoyed the laid-back lifestyle in the Keys. Don't get me wrong. Some of the businesses are as efficient as any watch designed in Switzerland, but many are more like some of the watches I've bought at a garage sale. They start out great but soon end up in the garbage or in another garage sale.

Back home, time is important to me. I work and have appointments that I try to maintain to the minute. In the Keys, the only time that really matters to me is the first of March when I am back on the road and heading home. Otherwise, I don't care whether it's 4:00 A.M. or 4:00 P.M.

A few minutes of sitting in the parking lot, and after listening to a few tunes on the radio, I was rewarded with lights being turned on in the store and the sight of Terry inside turning on the OPEN sign. Lighting up the windows, she headed to the front door and opened it while giving me her "Top O the morning to ya, Danny me boy."

A box of chum and four shrimp later, I headed back to camp and loaded my gear and supplies into my boat and headed out into the ocean.

My days in the Keys were about over. The sun's rays upon my face and the ocean's spray stinging my eyes and my flesh felt so wonderful that it left me a little sad knowing that I would be leaving soon. I think I would have blamed the saltwater in my eyes for the tears if I hadn't been alone. Whatever the reason, I was fine with my emotions.

I tell so many people I know or meet of the beauty of the ocean and the thrill of fishing in those waters. I think being alone on the ocean allows me the opportunity to reflect; it allows me a little time for introspection, or time to think about nothing at all. I drop some bait in the water and sit there waiting. An added bonus is a meal for later.

My time here was even more special than I had hoped for. I had found people I liked, and I think they might have felt the same way about me.

I realized in sharing a few days with Sam that life wasn't all about me or my customers and their needs. It was more about those I come into contact with, the moments shared with those people, and a better appreciation of life.

I came to the Keys hoping to write a book and catch some fish. I wound up realizing how special our lives truly can be when we take the time to enjoy everything and everyone we come into contact with.

The ocean provides not only food for the body, but she surrenders all she has to offer. If you succumb to that beauty, you'll be rewarded with food for the soul. Mother Nature provides sustenance for the body and will reap those benefits on anyone who accepts and looks beyond the obvious.

People, with all their idiosyncrasies, are what make life fun, and if you get outside of yourself and enjoy, it can be wonderful.

I spent the day fishing and caught more than enough for dinner, even a few for my loved ones back home. What I actually brought back home was a little food for my own soul and fodder for conversation for those I knew or had yet to meet.

Chapter 32

Mammals

The next morning arrived along with Sam (his friends had left), and we just sat there enjoying our coffee. We were probably on our third cup when Sam asked me if I had ever hunted deer.

I told him it had probably been ten or more years since the last time I sat in the woods hoping to kill something.

"Sam, I now have a house with a little bit of land in the suburbs. It really is amazing. I live less than ten minutes from downtown and maybe five minutes from the airport, yet I still have deer and turkeys in my yard. I used to hunt, and now I feed the bastards. I even let them eat my flowers. I enjoy watching them. I think I'm getting old and soft."

"Dan, I love bird hunting, but I've only tried 'mammal' hunting one time. I really didn't like it. In fact I hated it."

He also said (probably for the tenth time) that he had written an article that had been published in a magazine about hunting birds with a couple of dogs.

"Dan, my wife's father was a full bird Colonel in the Army, and he was in command of a base in North Carolina that I think was called Point Cherry. One time he asked if I would like to go hunting with him for deer. I readily accepted, but immediately after saying that I would, I wasn't happy with the thought of killing a deer or even hunting them. I did accept his invitation and wasn't about to tell him I wasn't really into that.

"A hunt was set up. In North Carolina it's legal to hunt deer with dogs. I was shown a spot to stay where it was thought that a deer might try to escape to, and the hounds were set loose."

Sam continued. His demeanor was kind of dejected, as if reliving the thought of killing a deer. "I was already into my disease to the point where I was taking naps frequently. I remember praying to a God I wasn't even sure existed, asking Him to not let any deer come by me.

"I nestled down into the place, and before long I was sleeping. A deer did come by and I hadn't even noticed. I was sound asleep. Someone in our group saw where that deer was going and knew where I was.

"After the hunt was over, he came up to me and was so pissed off that he started yelling at me. I think he was ready to set loose the hounds on me. He couldn't believe that I let a deer walk right by me without even firing a shot.

"The only thing that saved my ass from getting kicked by him was my father-in-law telling him, 'Stand down, soldier.' My father-in-law was the highest-ranking person on that base, and it was one of his subordinates who was so upset with me. It was the first and only time I ever attempted to hunt deer or any other mammal for that matter. I guess God was busy that day and didn't hear my prayers, probably with people who were praying for their team to win or their horse to come in, or their child to be cured."

Sam again mentioned his love of bird hunting and the article he had written. "Dan, I wrote this article and sent it off to a magazine. They actually liked it. I received a call from someone at that magazine. They wanted to publish it and offered me four hundred dollars. I told them six hundred sounded better, and he told me that four hundred was their one and only offer."

"I thought about it for a second and said, 'What, are you shitting me? It's yours.' I told him I would have given it to him for nothing and all he said was, 'I know.' Dan, I didn't care about the money."

I knew the feeling. When I was told my fishing story was in a local paper I had said the same thing: "What, are you shitting me?"

Sam said he'd written it before "spell check." He was not all that good at spelling, so he had kept his words simple. "Dan, I called back and asked if I could buy a few copies of that magazine and have them sent to me, and when I was asked how many I wanted, I said six. He told me they were mine and would be sent to me at no charge."

When I asked Sam why he didn't ask for a hundred copies, he said that he only had six friends at the time. "Now I'm down to two, Dan, and I'm really not so sure about you."

Sam had been keeping something next to him on the picnic table's bench and I hadn't noticed until he stood, picked it up, and placed it on the table between us: a copy of the magazine with his story.

I had never doubted that Sam had written that story. Why had he just now decided to share it with me? Maybe it had taken him this long to consider me worthy of his written words. Or maybe now that our time together here was almost over, he was going to put this wannabe writer in his place. Perhaps it had taken him this long to find it. Whatever the reason, the asshole had it all the time. He handed it to me and walked back to his campsite.

Here's Sam's story as it was originally published in the December/January 1998-99 issue of *Gun Dog* magazine.

* * *

Hunting With Two Clumbers

by Sam Catalano

A bird count of 12 roosters and 30 quail is consistent with the other hunts I've had at my friend Tom's ranch in eastern Washington State. I have been privileged to be invited to the ranch once a year for the last four seasons.

The players in this particular hunt were Tom and his two-year-old standard poodle, Katie; Tim and his five-year-old Lab, Kelly; Scott, an avid duck hunter; and me, along with my two Clumber spaniels, Sweetie and Buster, then about 4-1/2 and 2-1/2 years old, respectively.

The ranch is a working wheat ranch on which the owners take pride in providing habitat for wildlife. We encountered maize, lots of deep ditches with wild thorny olive trees, and large grass and tree strips between the wheat fields. The local pheasant population spends its leisure time trying to outsmart the coyotes and other predators looking for a tasty meal.

For those readers who don't know anything about Clumber spaniels, I will try to summarize my limited knowledge. They are the largest of the spaniels. Sweetie and Buster are typical at 60 and 65 pounds. They are powerful, short-legged dogs that look something like a large springer/Brittany cross.

There are about 1,500 Clumber spaniels in the U.S. and Canada. Although most of them are show dogs, there seems to be to a substantial amount of interest in hunting, hunt tests, and tracking events by Clumber spaniel clubs on both sides of the border. Both groups enthusiastically publish related material in club bulletins. Hunt tests have produced several senior hunters, and a couple of owners are hoping to deliver the first master hunter.

The dogs date back to the late 18th century and were originally monopolized by the British royalty. For many years the breed was confined to the kennels of a few noblemen in the neighborhood of Clumber. Some enthusiasts believe that the royalty's merciless culling of these dogs instilled the Clumber's unique hunting style, which is still obvious in the breed today.

The Clumber spaniel was brought to this continent as early as 1844 and was one of the first ten breeds recognized by the AKC when the organization was formed in 1884.

My Clumbers are relatively slow, thorough, persistent hunters that deliver their share of birds. My dogs have bright minds and excellent noses that are almost always at ground level; and they work the slightest scent. Generally, they hunt like a good Lab, only slower and closer. They—especially Buster—like to retrieve from land and water.

Physically, they are built to push through and crawl under heavy cover in ditches, draws and canyon breaks; and they much prefer this type of cover. Although effective, they are not graceful in an open field of wheat stubble. My dogs hunt with a consistent energy level that allows them to deliver a full day's hunt though the last day of a trip.

On the first morning of this hunt, I found myself jumping out of bed at just before first light and clanking around a strange kitchen trying to find the makings for that first cup of coffee. With cup in hand I wandered outside to take care of my dogs and was delighted to feel a blast of cold damp air hit my face. The ground was covered with frozen dew, the ranch was shrouded in a high fog, and a gentle breeze pushed early morning barnyard sounds to my ears. After mentally verifying a couple of those sounds to be pheasant cackles, 1 turned back into the house and, without any pity or pretense, terminated everyone's dreams.

As we left the house and crossed the road toward the first of a couple of six-acre maize fields, Tom laid out the plan. The Lab, the two Clumbers, and their respective owners were to work through the fields, pushing the birds toward the guys capping the ends. Tom knew that since I am a poor shot, I always try to avoid capping a field. I perform better with closer shots near my dogs; and, if the truth be known, I prefer watching my dogs work than actually shooting the birds.

As I watched Tom and Scott moving toward their posting positions, I noticed how well Katie, the poodle, was heeling next to Tom, and I wondered out loud, "Wouldn't it be nice if my dogs would do that?" Then my mind drifted back to last year when Katie individually flushed her first rooster for Tom's shot and retrieved it to his hand with a "Why didn't you say so?" look on her face. Tom was beyond happy.

Without warning, one of my white dogs flushed a hen pheasant, which startled me back into the present. Then Tim's Lab, Kelly, pushed up a couple of the quail which were unfortunate enough to zigzag in front of Tom's gun—he brought them down for his poodle to retrieve. Our dogs continued to flush a number of hen pheasants as we worked our way through the field. Just when I started to wonder if we were going to see any roosters, a huge cock bird magically appeared about maize-high, dazzling *me with color. About a microsecond later, a black Lab was in hot pursuit. Tim dropped it with his first shot.*

After another 40 yards, I witnessed two streaking lines, formed by the rustling tops of the maize, moving toward me from a 90-degree angle on a collision course. Those moving lines turned out to be Buster and Sweetie double-teaming a rooster that flushed so close to me that I had to look cross-eyed to see it. Then, with no time to think, I hit the bird with my first shot, and Buster retrieved it to hand.

Meanwhile, Kelly flushed some quail that angled toward Scott's gun. His talents as a duck shooter seemed to immediately transfer to his upland gun.

With 50 yards of maize remaining, I watched Sweetie rocket by me, ultimately flushing a big rooster toward Tom. It was moving high and fast as he swung hard while shooting. The bird hit the wheat stubble, running with an agile poodle in hot pursuit and gaining ground with each bounding stride. Moments later, while we were admiring the long spurs on Tom's rooster, the dogs gang-flushed another rooster out of the last few inches of cover. All we could do was watch it disappear behind a row of trees.

We left the first maize field and headed toward a muddy, flooded pasture. All four dogs were practically stepping on their tongues as they raced into the water. After a brief bath, a reasonably clean Sweetie and Buster ambled out of the water and immediately headed into a mudhole where they rolled and wallowed in the muck.

As I studied my short-legged, mud-covered hunting dogs with their noses always at ground level working the slightest scent, I couldn't help but think of the pigs that the French use to find truffles. My companions apparently had some of the same thoughts, but they didn't want to hurt my feelings by saying anything.

The remainder of the day produced lots of quail that the dogs rooted out one or two at a time. My shooting suffered, but thank God for the other guys. Watching Tom's poodle flush a quail, mark Tom's shot, and then retrieve the bird to his hand became mesmerizing for my dogs and me. My short-legged Clumbers didn't even try to outrun either the Lab or poodle for these long retrieves. They just kind of shrugged their shoulders, put their noses down, and kept flushing quail.

In the perfect light of late afternoon while hunting an island, I watched Buster and Sweetie get birdy at the tail end of a wooded area. They had something flanked and were moving it toward the edge of the island. Buster jumped in and flushed a rooster, which I shot. When the dogs didn't appear out of the cover to make a retrieve, I turned to watch them double team another rooster out of the same thick brush. My first shot was somewhere in the stratosphere, but my second shot either connected or the bird had a heart attack. Tim, who had witnessed the entire process, summed it up best when he said, "An almost true double is an almost true double." That was good enough for me.

As Scott, Tim, and I worked along a heavily covered ditch toward home, the dogs teamed up on one quail after another. Since these two guys were doing so well without me and I didn't want to ruin the afterglow of my "almost true double," I spent my time watching the dogs work. All three were in a frenzy when I began concentrating on Kelly, the Lab, who was obviously trying to outsmart an experienced rooster. Just when I thought that we had gone over the top of the bird, Kelly leaped three feet into the air, crashing down onto a bush. Out popped a freight train of a pheasant that Tim shot and Kelly retrieved.

With the sun setting in our faces, we dragged ourselves back to the ranchhouse. After a little tender loving care for our respective dogs, we headed into the house for dinner. Tom and Tim are excellent cooks; and we each feasted on a thick porterhouse with crushed garlic and cracked whole black peppers. Scott and I did a superb job of washing the dishes.

Much of our conversation was centered around dogs and embellished hunting and fishing stories. One notable segment was Tom's reply when he was asked what traits he looks for in his hunting dog. Tom, who has a son and daughter (seven and ten years old), listed the following requirements:

1: His dog must enjoy playing tea party with his daughter, which includes being dressed for the occasion.

2: When leaving the house for an early morning duck hunt, his dog must be able to jump out of his son's bed without waking the boy.

3: Everything else is gravy.

The weather the next morning was identical to the previous day. My excitement to start hunting was a bit tempered by the soreness of my body. So after my third cup of coffee, I beat the wake-up drum to get my friends moving.

The maize was not as good as it had been on the day before, but the ditches were productive for quail and pheasant. I even developed some intermittent skills at shooting quail.

We had some classic dog work and flushes in both the big deep ditches and grass strips between the wheat stubble. In one case the dogs were on a bird for about a third of a mile. When Buster and Kelly realized that the bird had doubled back on them, Kelly turned and hunted back toward us and Buster sprinted along the edge of the cover and turned back in at my feet.

These dogs worked toward each other and ultimately flushed the big rooster in tandem 20 yards in front of me. My first shot popped a wing. When the stunned bird hit the ground, it jumped up running hard. A very tired Buster was within 10 feet and slowly closed the gap. Just as Buster was leaping on this ground rocket, so were Kelly and Sweetie from opposite angles. After the collision all three dogs had the stunned expression of bighorn sheep after a butting.

As the dogs cleared their heads, the pheasant squeezed between them and never looked back. Fortunately, Katie had witnessed the scene from the top of a hill; she quickly chased down the bird and retrieved it from the tall grass.

With just a trace of the fog remaining, we left the ranch at noon and drove north to a somewhat more hilly area. I dropped my friends off at the head of a deep, two-mile-long ditch, and then backtracked so I could post the end of the ditch. By the time they arrived at my post, I was fast asleep but was prodded back to semi-consciousness by the smell of Kelly's breath in my face. Apparently they didn't need me because Scott had two roosters in his jacket and Tim and Tom had one each.

Our last stop of the hunt was along a creek with steep wild draw running at right angles. Without trace of fog to blur my vision, looked straight up at this steep hillside and was thankful that I had napped an hour ago.

My dogs love this type of cover and perform well in it. They hunted through the red brush, under the dense cover at the bottom of each draw, and in and along the creek. Two hours later we had flushed a few quail (I missed them), five hens, two deer but no roosters. Sundown was coming on fast, so we worked our way back to the cars and called it a hunt.

* * *

It was fun reading and gave me a little more insight to his character (I didn't need more).

To anyone that has never written a story before, or those that have, to have your first attempt accepted and put into print by a paper or magazine is really pretty cool. It's pretty damn exciting, yet Sam just left me alone with it.

I set down Sam's story. I loved the story, not only the way it was written but the way it portrayed Sam. It showed me that the person I had come to know as the humble person I believed he was. The only thing that he claimed to be good at was the cleaning of the dishes. All other accolades went to his friends and the dogs he so loved. He claimed to be a poor shot and even slept on his post while the others hunted. He didn't have to include that.

The fact was that, by then, he was in the eleventh year of his disease and he tired easily. I'm sure Huntington's was already taking away some of his coordination, yet his friends still trusted his judgment and had no problem with him shooting at moving targets, even though they were within range of his gun as well.

A little while later, he returned to ask what I thought and I said, "What, are you fucking nuts? This is wonderful!"

He also produced a couple of recipes he'd been telling me about that he wanted me to have, and I'd like to tell his hunting buddy Tim that for me it was a true "double."

I told Sam that maybe we should write a cookbook. "Sam, all we need is maybe thirty recipes. We'll call it *A Month of Cooking with Sam and Dan.*

Sam said that if we did it for the month of February, we'd only need twenty-eight. He came up with a title he liked even more. "Better yet, Dan, 'Eff oo let's cook.'"

And I came up with another. "EFF OO, let's cook with Dan and eat with Sam. Kitchen cooked by Dan and tasted and ingested by Sam."

We both laughed. Sam wanted to know why my name was first. I said that the food would have to be cooked before it could be eaten. He was okay with that. I told him that maybe I had finally come up with a business venture that we could go in on together.

My time here was over. I'd be leaving the next day, so Sam agreed to let me show him the oo in food and the eff in chef. That night I cooked come clam sauce over linguine, and he only said, "Eff oo, this is good."

We talked and said our goodnights. The following morning we shared our last cups of coffee together, and it was time for me to leave.

Sam's van having been sold, he would be flying back to Michigan and the independent-living apartment his sister had found for him.

Sam is a good man, and I hope I am a better man because of a few cups of coffee I shared with him. I had taken a few days out of my life to sit with another person and listen (to some degree) and found something I hadn't experienced in many years: a newfound friendship.

We all know what we've done, but to share our pasts with someone else and for them to do the same is to relive those experiences, both for ourselves and those we choose to open up to. Everyone should take a little time away from the self-imposed exile we find ourselves living in to experience people, to shut up and listen and even share: no TV, limited phone time, socialize with those we walk through life with and who we normally only exchange a few pleasantries with.

We all have our beliefs, but the only certain thing is that we'll all die. Take a few minutes of your life away from those you know and explore yourself and others. You just might find yourself while listening and experiencing others.

It's a nice concept, though most of us won't try, and those that do will go back to their mundane lives, but for a few it might open up a whole new world, the world of enjoying people and their memories and in doing so maybe creating a few of our own.

Chapter 33

Make Me an Angel

(Mama, Please Take Me Home)

After spending a few mornings with Sam, drinking coffee, and my writings not really going anywhere, I had told him that I wanted to try to write about him and asked if he was okay with that. I told him that the book that I had been trying to write, the one in my head, didn't seem all that important anymore.

"What, are you fucking nuts? Dan, I'd love that!"

Well, it wasn't the first time that someone had questioned my sanity, nor am I sure it will be the last.

As I'm prone to do, I procrastinated and wound up just enjoying the time we spent together, and my wannabe book fell by the wayside. I would take some notes as we sat and talked.

The writing wasn't really all that important at the time. I enjoyed our time and the fun I was having with Sam. It took a whole lotta more than a few years to complete this story of those days. I wrote it from the few notes I did take and from the memories he left me with.

I apologize for involving my own thoughts and my side of our conversations as much as I did. Sam said a lot more worthy things that were a part of our daily talks and which fell by the wayside, as did my note taking.

If it ain't all that accurate, so be it, though I do believe it's pretty damn close.

The most important thing I learned from Sam, and that I'd like to pass on to you, is to shut up and listen. Sam was liked by so many because he would listen to others. We already know what we have gone through in life. Although we may try to entertain (or brag), the stories we tell to others are nothing new to us. By listening, we allow *them* to relive their memories and to take us along for that ride down their memory lane, and we may in turn repeat those stories to others.

In the short time I have been coming here, I've heard stories told by others more than a few times. Sam must have heard them oh so many times more. He was always happy to sit and listen, even if he'd heard them before.

Sam loved to socialize. He would listen and ask questions and maybe share a few of his experiences. He lived in the moment, such a rare thing for most humans. Animals for the most part do just that. They only care about the now. Come autumn, they may store some food, but that's the extent of their future. How many people have you met in your life who would state so matter-of-factly, "There is nothing in my life that I would have changed."

Sam was the only person I have ever met, or probably ever will meet, who was content with the roads he had followed and the paths he had made. We would spend hours talking about anything and everything and nothing at all, sometimes just listening to the sounds around us.

I told Sam that he really had done a lot of fun things in his life, and he said, "Dan, everything I ever wanted to do, I did; every place I wanted to go to and see, I went to and experienced." This was spoken by a man who knew his days of doing what he wanted were numbered, and he accepted that. Even though he hoped for a cure, he doubted it would happen in his lifetime. He was realistic in what lay before him.

When his mother came to the point where she was bedridden and could only talk through her eyes, Sam listened to her as well. And she knew that she had passed down that deadly gene to him. He had developed a twitch, and he could see in her eyes that she knew it. He told her that he had just been working too much, that he was tired.

"Dan, I could never leave her with that guilt."

She also passed on to him the realization of how precious life can be, and Sam got that. I hope she knows what a beautiful gift she gave him, what a beautiful person she gave life to.

When he passes on, I'm sure that she will be there to tell him, "C'mon, Sam, it's time." She won't have to tell him a second time. Sam will embrace her and be ready.

I do hope that Sam knows that when a tree falls in the forest, it does make a sound and energy never dies.

Sometimes you just gots to believe.

Sam claimed to follow no religion, but he was, if not a better person, equal to all of the people I've met who claimed to be "God fearing and righteous." He followed his soul and no "Good Book" had to tell him right from wrong.

Everyone I've met in life has goals and dreams. Sam loved today because he knew that his tomorrows were coming to an end. He said that life had been good to him. Sam's life has been good to me as well. When I sit and listen, I am now amused by those who only want to talk. Whereas before I wanted to offer my two bits (two cents would be more appropriate), I now find myself listening a little more.

After Sam sold his vehicle and camper, he still came back, renting an efficiency in the campground for a month. I mentioned to a fellow camper that Sam was leaving the next day, and if they wanted to say goodbye, that he was just hanging out at his place. It was someone who had shared a little time with Sam and all they said was, "Oh I can't say goodbye, I feel so sorry for him."

How sad is it that some people care so much for others that they can't truly enjoy them because they feel sad for them.

Suck it up, people! Take friendships a step further.

Sam knew his future. It was the present that he enjoyed. It was all he knew he had, and so many missed out on those moments because they "felt sorry for him." Sam knew that most of his experiences were in the past. He knew everything about himself and was willing to share, but he was willing to listen, even though most people only wanted to talk about themselves. Hell, he *enjoyed* listening to others.

All our roads lead to the same destination: the grave. Yet there are so many paths to choose from to get to that place. Very few among us make new paths. We follow the roads of others. In a generation or two, we will be just a photo along with a story.

Maybe.

Sam stumbled along the same paths we all do, yet he took the time to enjoy everything he saw and everyone he came into contact with. Upon realizing that he had Huntington's disease, he lived with being able to see the end of his road, and he was in no hurry to get there. He walked slowly so that he could enjoy everything and everyone along the way.

Sam smelled the roses, and his roses were those he met along the roads of his life. For those willing to take the time to listen or share a few moments, he would spread a little of his manure and a whole lot of his sunshine on them that maybe would help them grow a little.

I got a whole lot of his manure and a whole lot of the sunshine that he radiated. Hopefully I can spread a little of his shit around as well.

If nothing else, I hope this story inspires someone to listen. There are so many people whose lives are filled with memories and who have no one to share them with. As our life is waning, the only things that we truly possess are a few memories. To share those brings joy to those who speak and more to those who actually listen.

Sam is now staying in independent living and we talk every week or so, and as for his fellow residents, he says, "Imagine living in a place with sixty of your grandparents."

Sam still made the best of it. He developed friendships, and one woman who was ninety years old would stop over at his room to smoke cigarettes. Sam was the only person still allowed to smoke in the whole complex (I think not only because it helped him, but because he was liked by so many). She would talk of the fling she was having with an eighty-eight-year-old who was also a resident there. (Gotta love it.)

I went to visit Sam and couldn't help but notice that he had a rather large blister on his nose. He told me that his hands didn't always do what his mind wanted, and instead of lighting a cigarette, he set his nose on fire.

I could only laugh.

He said that he was no longer able to bathe himself and those who worked there now did it for him. When I asked if he was embarrassed the first time, he said, "Hell no. I just got naked and into the shower and asked if the girls had ever seen a penis before. When they said they had, I said, 'Well, then wash away.' I bent over and spread my cheeks and they cleaned me up."

I had met a few of the people who worked there. They seemed like nice people and truly cared about Sam.

One of my favorite holidays is Mother's Day. I call everyone I know and wish them a "Happy Mother's Day," followed by a "Mother Fucker!" Sam was usually the first. On one particular day he didn't call back, and for weeks I kept leaving messages. Finally, his sister Margaret called and let me know that Sam was in a hospital, though doing okay. He was getting fluid in his lungs and they decided to keep him for six weeks.

I went to visit him after he got out.

"Dan, they decided I needed physical rehabilitation, and for six weeks they beat the snot out of me. They really beat me up. I know what they were doing was helping, and I know it made me better physically, but I was to the point that I finally told them I had had enough and either they release me or I was going to walk out."

The rehab must have done a whole lot of good because Sam's speech was so much better than it had been in our conversations. He was using a walker to get around. He accepted that. In that time he wasn't allowed to smoke, and after leaving rehab never did again.

I returned to the Keys, trying to continue writing these memoirs. Needing a break from writing and trying to recall our time together, I went to Key West to jog a few memories. It was Ash Wednesday. A priest was on the steps of a cathedral on Duvall Street, where almost everyone walking by had had a cocktail or two. He stood on those steps and placed ashes upon the foreheads of any who wished to be annointed.

I walked up to him and said, "Father, I was raised in the Catholic Church, though I no longer follow its teachings, and would be considered a sinner by those teachings, but if you would bless me, I would appreciate it."

He looked at me and said, "My son, we are all sinners and you are already blessed." Then he whispered to me, "Now get the fuck off my steps." (Just kidding about that last part.)

I am a selfish person in that I wish I was still sharing my morning coffee with Sam. I know he is doing fine. Energy never dies, and Sam had a soul that had nothing to regret in this life.

I don't know a lot other than a tree falling in the forest with no one around does make a sound, and that a good person doesn't need a religion to show him "the way."

The last time I went to see Sam in his "home," he wanted to go to a Japanese restaurant that he liked and asked me to shave him and help him get some clean clothes on. All spiffed up I loaded both him and his walker into my car. Our waiter was an older Japanese man that stood not far from us, pretending to be busy (though watching us), making sure everything was in order. When Sam would drop something on the table, this gentleman would come over and clean it up. Sam spilled some food onto his lap and the man asked if he could clean that up and did so as well. It was such a simple act of kindness, yet the beauty of a stranger doing this remains in my mind.

Sam, using his walker, walked along beside me going to my car and it was *I* that put my hand on *his* shoulder as we walked together.

Later in the day he went to bed. I was lying on the couch in the other room and I heard him calling out, "Ma mmm ma Mama Ma MAMA." I looked in on him still sleeping and wondered if she was calling him home, or maybe he was asking her. But I guess it wasn't time. In the morning we shared coffee.

In writing this story, these memories, I relive our time together, and it is usually in the middle of the night when I write them.

I cry from this gift within,
As my life flows through this pen,
Both tears of joy and sorrow,
As I live my past again.
It is my teardrops that you have read.

I do believe the next time it was Sam's mom who called to him. She didn't have to call him again.

* * *

Thanks, buddy. I love you. I hope I am doing well in this life.

In memory of
Samuel D. Catalano
8/2/1945–10/17/2016

Epilogue

The Serb

I have continued going to the Keys and have moved even deeper into the bowels of the campground.

I have moved past the fish cleaning station and now reside in The Dark Side.

I've a new neighbor, whose name is Nick, and he refers to our little strip in that section as "Rummy Row" He is of Serbian descent and I call him "Nickolai the Serb."

Most mornings we sit and drink coffee, sometimes a few cocktails at night, and exchange memories and a few thoughts.

Nick has a love of fly fishing and hunting birds that have been flushed by dogs. He even seems to enjoy my cooking and I enjoy his as well. I think I am going to like Nick.

I made a bet with "Horny Bill" (last name Harless) and he lost. "Harless, where's my nickel!"

There was a pelican in the campground with a broken wing and someone from the Key West wildlife center came to its rescue, and a few of us helped in its capture. I had shared my writings with Bruce and his wife... and he looked at me and said, "I hear pelican tastes just like eagle."

Diane and Gary were walking by and stopped to say hello. They were friends of both Sam and me and were from Michigan. I asked them, "So what do you people from Michigan call yourselves, Michigonians or Michiganites, Michiganders?" Diane shook her head as she continued on.

"You know, Gary, you have a lovely wife. The only thing I can see wrong with her is she must be a poor judge of character."

And so the memories live on.

And energy never dies.

Afterward

The Ugly Truth

I think I have portrayed my friendship with Sam in a fun way, in the way that it was in the time we spent together.

Sam used to say to me that if a woman wanted to be involved with him, he would have to ask himself just what was wrong with her. I didn't get it. Sam was fun; he loved everything and everyone. I thought that to not want to be around him was to miss out on a good thing. I didn't understand why he would say that, until the last time I saw him.

Huntington's disease is inherited. The actual name is Huntington's Chorea. Sam only called it Huntington's, as I have throughout this book. The only way a person will get this disease is from a parent who has it.

Huntington's Chorea will gradually take away the mind's ability to tell your body what to do. It is gradual, yet the mind left intact realizes.

A parent who raised you and loved you is watched as they slowly succumb to this disease and die. They did not know they had it until long after the birth of their children. Once they know, they live in fear that they may have passed it on. There is only a chance of it.

The first time I sat with Sam and we talked, he said to me that he was too selfish of a person to have any children. I told him I thought otherwise.

Within Sam's family, Huntington's disease has probably ended due to his being "selfish" and wanting to enjoy just himself and his life. Sam was probably the most caring person I have met, and the last time I saw him I realized why he wouldn't let a woman fall in love with him. Huntington's leaves a person not even realizing that they are standing and urinating on the floor. Sam looked at me standing there, and I realized why he remained single. He cared too much about others to think of himself. He had foreseen his future through the demise of his mother. It was not an end that he wished to share.

I slept on Sam's couch and I would hear him call out "Mama" in his sleep. I really believed that he was ready to move on and asking her to help.

Sam had foreseen his destiny through the fate of his mother. The last time I saw Sam, I understood.

Sam rarely spoke of his wife or of why she left. I never asked. In knowing Sam I have to wonder if he was experiencing signs, and in knowing that he had this disease, he might have even encouraged her. He was that good a man.

Apologies

To my customers, those who trust me and my work: I have a business card that says "prompt and reliable." A customer brought me to task on that statement and all I could say was that he should rid himself of that card, that it was old. The new ones say, "I hope to get there sooner or later." My book—a memoir I'm told—has kinda consumed both me and my time, and I have not always been true to the "prompt" part.

To those in Electric: We aren't all bad people down here that manage to do without all the modern amenities of the life that has been offered to us by modern science.

To the fools of the world who think they can find creativity by going someplace: Creativity will find you if it's meant to be. You just have to learn to... sit and listen to your soul. You don't have to discover yourself. Life is about creating yourself.

To those that adhere to being "green": I have discovered the computer, and many trees will not be sacrificed due to my lack of finding the right words the first time, although I will still be chopping down a few for my customers.

To those that adhere to another's "belief": Religions need followers and sometimes you get in your own god's way.

To Sam: I know that the words I have written pale in comparison to what you have given me in our friendship. I hope they came close enough that those who read them will at least somewhat understand.

To my liver: I seem to find the right words after a few drinks. I hope you are ready for another round because I have another story in my head. There is a really big fish out there that needs to be written about.

To Toe-mas: He is just a figment of my imagination, a case of writer's block gone wild... maybe.

To you who have read this book, I have made a thousand corrections. I don't have it in me to go through it again.

I chop wood for a living this writing stuff is new to me.

I think or rather hope I did good.

Daniel P. Hochreiter

About the author

Dan was born in the town of Gates, a western suburb of the greater metropolis of Rochester, New York. He graduated from the learned institute of Gates Chili .

He graduated with a degree in.... a most prestigious degree in, a most accomplished degree in......

Aww hell he got a high school diploma.

A good work ethic and a bit of common sense has helped him do okay in life.

It has to be through genetics because being the seventh child (the baby of the bunch) of a working class family he was spoiled rotten.

Go figure!

Made in the USA
Columbia, SC
14 December 2017